BANAN.
AND OTHER PLAYS

DON NIGRO

SAMUEL FRENCH

FOUNDED 1830

SAMUELFRENCH.COM

ISBN   978-0-573-63221-1   Printed   in   U.S.A.   #4252

MUSIC USE NOTE

Licensees are solely responsible for obtaining formal written permission from copyright owners to use copyrighted music in the performance of this play and are strongly cautioned to do so. If no such permission is obtained by the licensee, then the licensee must use only original music that the licensee owns and controls. Licensees are solely responsible and liable for all music clearances and shall indemnify the copyright owners of the play and their licensing agent, Samuel French, Inc., against any costs, expenses, losses and liabilities arising from the use of music by licensees.

**IMPORTANT BILLING AND CREDIT
REQUIREMENTS**

All producers of *BANANA MAN AND OTHER PLAYS* must give credit to the Author of the Play in all programs distributed in connection with performances of the Play, and in all instances in which the title of the Play appears for the purposes of advertising, publicizing or otherwise exploiting the Play and/or a production. The name of the Author *must* appear on a separate line on which no other name appears, immediately following the title and *must* appear in size of type not less than fifty percent of the size of the title type.

CONTENTS

BANANA
MAN

CHARACTERS

SAM, a tall Irish writer
BUSTER, an old actor
WAITRESS, a young woman

SETTING

An Italian restaurant in Greenwich Village in the summer of 1964. All we see is a round table with a checkered table cloth and Buster's dinner on it: spaghetti and meatballs, garlic bread, a jar of grated cheese and a bottle of beer.

In New York, in the summer of the year 1964, Alan Schneider directed a small film written by Samuel Beckett and featuring Buster Keaton. In the evenings, they would have dinner in an Italian restaurant, Beckett and Schneider and the rest at one table, Buster by himself at another. This is probably not what happened there.

The playwright wishes to thank the good people at Ensemble Studio Theatre in New York, Lawrence Harbison of Samuel French Inc., and Joseph Nigro.

(An Italian restaurant in Greenwich Village, New York, in the summer of 1964. BUSTER, an old actor, is eating spaghetti and meatballs and drinking beer. In the background, we hear, faintly, the sound of 'Vesti la giubba,' from Leoncavallo's Pagliacci as we watch BUSTER eat. Music begins to fade as SAM, a tall Irish writer, walks over to BUSTER'S table, holding his own beer bottle and glass. BUSTER eats.)

SAM. Do you mind the company? *(BUSTER shrugs, shakes his head no, indicates chair. Sam puts his bottle and glass down and sits. Pause. BUSTER eats. SAM watches.)* Good spaghetti? *(BUSTER nods, drinks beer from his bottle, and continues to eat.)* I had the ravioli. Also good. *(Pause.)* Alan thought perhaps you might have questions.
BUSTER. Alan?
SAM. Yes.

(Pause.)

BUSTER. Who's Alan?
SAM. The director.
BUSTER. Oh. *(Pause.)* About what?
SAM. About the film.

(Long pause. BUSTER eats spaghetti. SAM waits.)

BUSTER. The monkey.

(Pause.)

SAM. Yes?
BUSTER. The woman with the monkey.
SAM. Yes. *(Pause.)* What is the question?

7

BUSTER. I don't like monkeys. First wife had a monkey. Monkeys shit everywhere.

(BUSTER drinks beer from the bottle. Pause.)

SAM. You want the monkey cut?
BUSTER. No.

(Pause. BUSTER eats.)

SAM. I'm a great admirer of your work, you know.

(Pause.)

BUSTER. Is there any more cheese in that thing?

(SAM passes the jar of grated cheese. BUSTER puts some on his spaghetti. A young WAITRESS appears.)

WAITRESS. So, is everybody doing okay here?
BUSTER. Uh huh.
WAITRESS. Do you need more cheese?
BUSTER. I have never in my life had too much cheese.
WAITRESS. Okay. *(To SAM.)* Would you like anything, else, sir?
SAM. A ticket to France.
WAITRESS. Pardon?
SAM. I'm fine, thank you.
WAITRESS. *(Looking at BUSTER.)* Excuse me, but I know you, don't I?
BUSTER. Nobody knows me.
WAITRESS. I do. Really. The minute you walked in, I felt sure I knew you, but I can't figure out from where. Do you know me?
BUSTER. I don't know anybody.
WAITRESS. Are you sure?
BUSTER. I'd remember you, dear.
WAITRESS. Oh, that's sweet. You're a sweetheart.
BUSTER. *(Gesturing towards SAM with a piece of garlic bread.)* Do you know him?
WAITRESS. *(Looking at SAM.)* No. I don't think so. Uh oh. My boss is giving me dirty looks. Got to go pretend I'm working. I'm sure I

know you. Don't tell me. I'll figure it out.

(The WAITRESS goes.)

    BUSTER. Nobody knows writers.
    SAM. Yes. That's the beauty of it.
    BUSTER. In Hollywood, writers are lower than dirt.
    SAM. Things are the same everywhere. .
    BUSTER. Except Hollywood is nowhere.
    SAM. Everywhere is nowhere.
    BUSTER. Hollywood is both.

(Pause. BUSTER eats.)

    SAM. You don't like Hollywood?
    BUSTER. *(Shrugs.)* Shut up and play cards. That's my philosophy.
    SAM. Marcus Aurelius.
    BUSTER. Roscoe Arbuckle. *(He drinks some beer.)* You play poker?
    SAM. No.

(Pause. BUSTER eats. The WAITRESS returns with more cheese.)

    WAITRESS. More cheese. You're an actor, right?
    BUSTER. No. I'm in the movies.
    WAITRESS. Really? I wish I was. I mean, I want to be. I aspire to that. But first I want to learn my craft on the stage, you know? Just until I make enough money to move to Hollywood. Hollywood is my dream. What do you do in the movies?
    BUSTER. Mostly I play poker with dead people.
    WAITRESS. *(To SAM.)* He's kidding. He's an actor, isn't he?
    SAM. A very great one.
    WAITRESS. I was going to say Moe, from the Three Stooges, but that's not right. Wait, don't tell me. I'll get it.I'm very good at this, re-ally.

(The WAITRESS goes.)

    BUSTER. Wrong stooge. *(He drinks some beer, eats.)* The thing about writers is, a movie isn't words.
    SAM. No.

BUSTER. When they put in words, it was all down hill from there.
SAM. I agree.
BUSTER. Yeah?
SAM. Absolutely.
BUSTER. But you're a writer.
SAM. Yes.
BUSTER. Words are what you're made of.
SAM. No.
BUSTER. And you're Irish. The Irish are made of words.
SAM. The Irish are made of disappointment.
BUSTER. Who isn't?

(BUSTER eats. The WAITRESS returns.)

WAITRESS. Are you two, like, an old vaudeville team?
SAM. I believe you've found us out.
WAITRESS. I knew it. I could tell. I've seen you on the Ed Sullivan show, right?
BUSTER. Could be.
WAITRESS. Are you the guys who pull the little train? And, you know, wear like fourteen suits of clothes and come up with all kinds of fruit and flowers out of your pockets and things? Except I think there's only one of that guy. He hums this little falsetto song while he pulls all these weird things out of his pockets and makes these little weird falsetto exclamations of joy and wonder when he finds something really remarkable in his pocket, like hundreds of bananas and pineapples or something, and takes off about four hundred layers of clothes and then makes this little train out of them and at the end drives off in the train blowing a whistle in his long johns. Do you know that guy?
BUSTER. You're thinking of the Banana Man.
WAITRESS. That's who it is. So you're not the Banana Man?
SAM. Actually, I'm the Banana Man.
WAITRESS. Really? I'm a great admirer of your work.
SAM. Thank you.
WAITRESS. But if you're the Banana Man, then who is he?
BUSTER. I'm the banana.
WAITRESS. You guys are pulling my leg, aren't you?
BUSTER. In my dreams.
WAITRESS. Don't tell me. I'll get it. *(She goes, speaking as she does to somebody off.)* Yeah, yeah, I'm coming. Keep your pants on,

Guido.

BUSTER. In vaudeville my father used to mop up the stage with me. I mean, literally. Sewed a valise handle to the back of my coat and swung me around in a circle, and then he'd let go, and I'd go flying off into the air.

SAM. Wasn't that dangerous?

BUSTER. For the audience. Then he'd attach a mop handle to my belt and use me to mop the floor. I was a big sensation in nineteen eight. Well, it was a slow year. Then the child welfare people got wind of it and Pop was in deep shit.

SAM. Did they take you away?

BUSTER. Naw. We had to go to this welfare lady's office for an interview, and I spent the whole time juggling her apples and hanging upside down from the ceiling fan. Then I stripped naked to show her I had no bruises. Dad offered to strip, too, but only if she would first, and while she was still sputtering and making these little whooping noises we skipped town and did the circuit in Nebraska. At last, the big time.

SAM. And the rest is history.

BUSTER. If that's what you want to call it. *(Pause. Thoughtful as he eats.)* Can I wear my hat?

SAM. In the restaurant?

BUSTER. In the movie. Can I wear my porkpie hat? I always feel better in my hat.

(Pause.)

SAM. I think the hat would be fine.

BUSTER. Good. *(Pause.)* I'm sorry about that other thing.

SAM. What other thing? You mean the monkey?

BUSTER. No, that thing with the boots.

SAM. Boots?

BUSTER. And the Russian guy who's got to take a leak.

(Pause.)

SAM. *Waiting for Godot.*

BUSTER. Maybe. That play where nothing happens in the first act and then in the second act nothing also happens. It was nice you asked if I was available to do it.

SAM. I was sorry you weren't.

BUSTER. Actually, I've been available since about nineteen twenty-nine, I just didn't get it. The play. It didn't make any damn sense to me at all. Of course, neither does this goddamned movie, but now I really need the dough. *(Pause.)* So, who did you ask first?

SAM. Who did I ask what?

BUSTER. I know I wasn't the first choice for this thing. I haven't been anybody's first choice since before Herbert Hoover, who was not my first choice, either.

SAM. Alan wanted Charlie Chaplin.

BUSTER. Umm hmm. Then who?

SAM. Zero Mostel.

BUSTER. Who?

SAM. Zero Mostel. Then Jack MacGowran.

BUSTER. Who the hell are these people?

SAM. Very talented individuals who were not available. Unless of course it just didn't make any damned sense to them, either.

BUSTER. In other words, I was the pickle at the bottom of Alan's barrel.

SAM. You were floating at the top of mine.

(Pause. BUSTER drinks. The WAITRESS returns.)

WAITRESS. Did you used to be in horror movies?

BUSTER. You're thinking of Boris Karloff. He's taller and better looking.

WAITRESS. No, not him. The one who plays the organ. Do you know the one I mean?

SAM. Buxtehude?

WAITRESS. No.

BUSTER. With or without a monkey?

WAITRESS. The guy who played the organ in the sewer.

BUSTER. Lon Chaney.

WAITRESS. You mean the wolf man?

BUSTER. No. The wolf man was Junior. The organ player in the opera sewer was Senior.

WAITRESS. So you're Lon Chaney Senior?

BUSTER. If I am, I've been dead even longer than I thought I was.

WAITRESS. You're not dead.

BUSTER. Tell that to Darryl Zanuck. No, wait, maybe he's dead, too. Actually, everybody I know is dead. I play poker with four of the deadest people in Hollywood, and the hell of it is, they still beat me.

WAITRESS. How can they beat you if they're dead?

BUSTER. They cheat. In Hollywood, even the dead are screwing you over. Some of the crookedest people in Hollywood have been dead a long time.

WAITRESS. All right. I give up. Who are you?

SAM. He's Buster Keaton.

WAITRESS. *(Looking at BUSTER.)* No, I don't think so.

SAM. Yes, he is.

WAITRESS. Buster Keaton is a little boy with a Prince Valiant hair-cut and an ugly dog who sells shoes.

BUSTER. That's Buster Brown.

WAITRESS. Oh, that's right. Sorry. Is my face red?

BUSTER. I like a girl with a red face. I like a girl with a red any-thing. I like a girl who isn't dead. You're not dead. I find that incredibly attractive in a woman. If I wasn't a very happily married man I'd pick you up, take you down the sewer and play my organ for you.

WAITRESS. You're really Buster Keaton?

BUSTER. I can't deny it. Unless you're with the Internal Revenue people. Then I'm Rudolph Valentino.

WAITRESS. *(Looks at him for a long moment, then:)* No you're not.

(The WAITRESS goes.)

BUSTER. And there you have it. The president of my fan club. *(He drinks out of the bottle.)* So, if I was floating at the top of your pickle barrel, how come you let them ask all those other guys first?

SAM. I thought you were dead.

BUSTER. Ah. *(Pause.)* So did I.

(BUSTER resumes eating. Pause. SAM watches him, thoughtful.)

SAM. The purpose of the monkey is to anticipate the behavior of the small dog and the large cat later, that is, focussing upon the object, you, and ignoring the observing eye, which is also the camera. The creatures are not self aware. But you are. They focus upon others, not upon the observing eye, which is actually you observing yourself, although we don't know that until the end.

(Pause.)

BUSTER. Uh huh. *(Pause.)* It's a set up.

SAM. It's a set up.

BUSTER. But what's the joke?

SAM. There is no joke, exactly.

BUSTER. No kidding. Although I do like the bit with putting out the dog and the cat comes in and then putting out the cat and the dog comes in and then putting out the dog and the cat comes in. That's a good bit. Fatty Arbuckle did that bit.

SAM. Did he?

BUSTER. Steal from the best, I always say. *(Pause.)* So why does this guy have a nail in his head?

SAM. Well—

BUSTER. Never mind. I don't really want to know.

SAM. Did Fatty Arbuckle have a nail in his head?

BUSTER. No, he had a dead girl in his bathtub.

SAM. Ah. The corpse in the bathtub. Petronius did that bit.

BUSTER. Who?

SAM. Friend of Zero Mostel.

BUSTER. Oh. *(Pause.)* He got a bum rap, you know. Roscoe Arbuckle. He was a very nice man. Never hurt a fly. And a great comedian. So they destroyed him. These people. They're like hyenas. Those sons of bitches get every single goddamned one of us in the end. They'll get you, too. Just wait. God damned sons of bitches.

(BUSTER stares at his beer morosely. Pause.)

SAM. You know, Buster, it's probably time we were getting you back to your hotel. We start shooting pretty early in the morning, and it's going to be awfully hot tomorrow.

BUSTER. Never missed a call in my life. Let me ask you something, Sid.

SAM. Sam.

BUSTER. Let me ask you something, Sam. Just between us, just what the hell is this goddamned pretentious fucking piece of horseshit really supposed to be about, anyway? I mean, there's a monkey, and a parrot, and a goddamned fish, and this poor son of a bitch is covering up the mirrors and walking around with a nail in his head. I mean, Jesus Christ. What the hell IS this shit?

(Pause.)

SAM. Well. If to be is to be perceived, then the way not to be is not to be perceived, but even if others are not perceiving one, one is still relentlessly and hopelessly perceiving one's self, and in doing so is perpetuating the agony of being. So in a sense what you are doing is attempting to escape from the relentless perception of yourself. But, of course, you fail.

(Pause.)

BUSTER. I fail.
SAM. Yes.

(Pause.)

BUSTER. Well, that I know how to do. I lost everything I had to a bunch of dead guys. Let me give you a tip, Sid. Always write your own material. And don't let the sons of bitches mess with it, no matter what it costs you. The thing every asshole in the universe wants more than anything else is to fuck up what somebody else made. When I lost control of my movies, I lost everything. Now I'm reduced to doing gasoline commercials and pretentious crap like this. No offense. It might be crap, but at least it's your crap. Anybody wants to try and talk you into getting rid of that damned monkey, you just tell them to stuff it up their ass. And take it from me, nobody wants a monkey up their ass. I think Fatty Arbuckle used to do that bit, but he gave it up. Never work with animals. Animals shit everywhere. Roscoe worked with a dog once, and gave the dog all the laughs. He was a real artist. Me, I'm the Invisible Man. I got no more reflection.

(BUSTER drinks, then stares at his plate. Pause.)

WAITRESS. *(Returning, yelling back in the direction she's come from.)* Well, all right then, Guido. You can just take your stupid job and stuff it in your goddamned sawdust and rat shit ravioli. *(To SAM and BUSTER.)* Take my advice, don't ever order the ravioli. Guido's ravioli is like life. It tastes good as long as you don't look too close at what it's made of, but it's a trick. It's all a trick. *(She puts her hands out, a little wobbly.)* Woops. There goes the world.

SAM. *(Steadying her with his hand.)* Are you all right?

WAITRESS. Sure. I'm fine. I'm just going blind.

BUSTER. Sit down here, sweetheart.

(SAM and BUSTER help the WAITRESS sit on the chair between them.)

WAITRESS. *(Bouncing up again immediately.)* Hey. Was that somebody's hand on my ass?

BUSTER. Shame on you, Sid.

SAM. Don't look at me.

BUSTER. *(Retrieving his squashed hat from the chair where she's sat on it.)* It was just my hat.

(BUSTER puts the hat on the table, and they sit her down again.)

WAITRESS. Actually it felt pretty good. Don't worry, I always go blind when I get really pissed off. It irritates my sinuses, and they push on my optic nerve and everything goes dark for a minute or so. Wow, what a day. I get fired, go blind, and then some guy's hat feels me up.

BUSTER. And you met Moe from the Three Stooges.

WAITRESS. Yeah. That was the best part.

SAM. I hope your conversations with us weren't a contributing factor to you losing your job. If you'd like me to speak with the manager—

WAITRESS. Oh, no, fuck him. I get fired all the time. I think it's because I have an artistic temperament, you know? I need a drink.

BUSTER. Here. Have some of Sid's beer.

WAITRESS. Okay. Thank you, Sid. *(She drinks from SAM'S bottle.)* I can see again. It's a miracle. God bless Ballantine Beer. See, if you have an artistic temperament, like I do, you have a lot of nervous breakdowns, and living in this city makes everybody a little squirrely after a while. It's like somebody is always looking at you, you know? In the street, in the buildings, even in my apartment, I keep getting this feeling somebody is out there with binoculars or a telescope spying on me when I run around naked like on the way to the shower or in the shower or on the way out of the shower or just for the hell of it, do you know what I mean? Although, I guess a person wants to be an actor because they like being looked at, I suppose that's part of it, but it can't be all of it. I mean, there's got to be something else that makes you give up having a real life in order to take on these, like, other identities, you know what I mean? I guess I do like being looked at, sort of, but I also resent it. It's like I want the audience to love me, but also secretly I hate them for gaping at me. It's like I need to do this thing because I'm so lonely, you know, and yet, the process of doing it seems to separate me more, in a way, you know, from, like, real life. Am I making any sense here? Do you want that meatball? I haven't had anything to eat today but a couple of Fig Newtons and a Dilly Bar.

BUSTER. Be my guest.

WAITRESS. Thank you. *(She stabs the meatball with his knife and eats it like a corndog.)* Actually I'm a vegetarian, but I've got this thing about meatballs, I just can't seem to say no to Italian food. It's what God must eat in Heaven, you know? Him and the angels, every night, sneaking into the refrigerator after midnight and pigging out on lasagna and fresh bread with butter.

SAM. Well, we learn from Dante that they speak Italian in Heaven. I suppose it's only one step farther to imagine them eating meatballs.

WAITRESS. Of course, if there's meatballs in heaven they'd have to be made out of meat that had never actually been real cows or pigs or anything that could look back at you, you know?

SAM. Magic meatballs.

WAITRESS. Exactly. Unlike this meatball, which is however incredibly good, even though I know for a fact that at least half of this thing must be old shredded newspapers and the other half was once somebody's mother. Can I have the rest of this garlic bread?

BUSTER. Absolutely.

WAITRESS. Thanks. You're a peach, Moe. I should have known this was going to be a bad day because last night I dreamed a house fell on me. I must be really messed up, huh?

SAM. Not at all. LeFanu used to dream that all the time.

WAITRESS. Lefty who?

SAM. Joseph Sheridan LeFanu. Irish writer. He kept dreaming he was walking in a strange part of Dublin at night, and he came to an old house, and looked up, and realized it was about to collapse on him.

BUSTER. I've done that.

WAITRESS. You dreamed a house fell on you, too?

BUSTER. No. I actually had a house fall on me.

WAITRESS. Is that what happened to your hat?

BUSTER. Yes.

WAITRESS. Can I try it on?

BUSTER. Are you over eighteen?

WAITRESS. Yes.
BUSTER. All right.
WAITRESS. Cool.

(The WAITRESS puts on BUSTER'S hat.)

WAITRESS. This is a great hat. Why does it smell like molasses?
BUSTER. I put molasses on my hat to attract beautiful women.
WAITRESS. Does it work?
BUSTER. You're here, aren't you?
WAITRESS. Well, yes.
BUSTER. There you go.
WAITRESS. But I wasn't attracted by the molasses.
BUSTER. Then what was it? The meat balls?
WAITRESS. It think it was the sadness.
BUSTER. It's not wise to be attracted to sadness.
WAITRESS. I'm not attracted to all sadness. Just a certain kind of sadness. I don't know. I can't explain it. I had a dog once who looked at me the way you do.
BUSTER. So I remind you of your dog?
WAITRESS. In a way. And I mean that totally as a compliment.
BUSTER. I'll take it.
WAITRESS. So were you killed, when this house fell on you?
BUSTER. Yes. I was.
SAM. It was in a movie. He set it up so the whole side of a house would fall all around him, but he stood in a particular spot so when it fell, the open window of the house would fall directly over the spot where he was standing.
WAITRESS. But it was actually, like, trick photography, right? Because all that stuff is really a trick, you know. Like an optical illusion.
SAM. No. It wasn't a trick. He planned it all very carefully. He stood there and the whole side of the house fell and the open window came down just where he wanted it to and when it was over, he was the only thing left standing. It was incredibly brave. Only a real artist would be that brave.
BUSTER. Or that stupid.
WAITRESS. Wait a minute. I saw that. I know who you are.
BUSTER. Don't tell me. I don't want to know.
WAITRESS. I saw you on television when I was a little girl. You were doing Romeo and Juliet.

BUSTER. Which one was I?

WAITRESS. Actually you were both of them. It was the balcony scene. And there was a balcony.

BUSTER. Clearly a big budget production.

WAITRESS. No, it was this big empty stage in a big old theatre with just a balcony with a ladder in back, and some fake bushes down below, and the theatre was all dark, but you could hear people laughing from somewhere, it was actually pretty spooky, and you'd be Romeo down in the fake bushes, wearing this silly hat, and then you'd run behind the balcony thing and climb up the ladder and put on this wig and answer yourself as Juliet, and then you'd run down the ladder and back into the bushes and do Romeo, and then you'd run around back and up the ladder and put on the wig and do Juliet, with this wonderfully silly falsetto voice—

BUSTER. You're sure this wasn't Laurence Olivier?

WAITRESS. No, it was you. It was the most amazing thing I ever saw. It was like—it explained the whole world to me, as a child, you know? I mean, you're trapped in this theatre, in this play, this performance, and you don't know what the hell you're doing, and you're like horribly miscast, in way over your head, and you can hardly even remember your lines, and you're stuck in these stupid costumes and this creaky, flabby, farty, falling apart old wreck of a body—no offense—but you keep running up that goddamned ladder anyway, and yanking your costumes on and off, and playing your characters for all you're worth, and you can hear the laughter in the dark, but you don't know for sure whether anybody's actually out there watching or not, and you don't even know if they're laughing with you or at you, or what, but you just keep on playing your action. I mean, you couldn't really see for sure. Maybe there wasn't anybody out there in the dark at all, maybe it was just a laugh track somebody had left on and then went away and never came back, or got switched on accidentally when a pigeon landed on it or something. Your life could be like a movie playing in a empty theatre, for all anybody knows. But part of the reason we keep playing our part anyway is that we have this eerie, irrational feeling that somebody is looking at us, you know, that somebody is watching us who's at least interested enough in what happens to keep watching, and that's like really horrifying, almost as horrifying as looking in the mirror, and yet, in a way, that's what keeps us alive, the fact that maybe somebody is watching.

BUSTER. Who? Who's watching us?

WAITRESS. I don't know. The audience.

BUSTER. What audience? Where do they come from? Where do they go?

WAITRESS. We don't know. It could be anybody. It could be a gazillion people, it could be just one person, it could be us looking at ourselves in a mirror, it could be nobody.

BUSTER. Godot.

WAITRESS. Who?

BUSTER. Friend of Sid's. You wait around for him but he doesn't come.

WAITRESS. Could be him. Could be Jack the Ripper. We just don't know. But there we are, standing around backstage in this big old theatre, and we think we hear our cue, so we rush out onto the stage, and when we get out there, we think we can hear them rustling around in the dark, shifting in their seats and farting, and maybe a cough, or a titter, or something, and we know we've got to do something, so finally we start doing Shakespeare or old vaudeville routines or we just take off all our clothes and dance around naked, we pretend we're somebody else, who is actually us, because everybody is inside us, because we're inside everybody else. That's what it meant to me, when I saw you going up and down that ladder. Like the whole world in a little glass paper weight. It was totally absurd. And absolutely true. It was the truest thing I ever saw in my life. It was great. You were great. And that's what made me know for sure I had to be in the theatre. It changed my life forever. Buster Keaton. You're Buster Keaton. Thank you.

(Pause.)

BUSTER. How much do I owe you for the spaghetti?

SAM. No, I'll pay.

WAITRESS. That's okay. This one's on me.

SAM. But you can't afford that. You've just been fired.

WAITRESS. Oh, he fires me every night. Look at him over there sulking behind that stupid mustache. There's nobody to wait on the tables now. He never thinks ahead. He's got the brain of a cheese log, but he needs me, you know? It's good to be needed. It gives you the illusion that somebody's out there in the dark. *(Calling over to the invisible Guido in the darkness.)* Yeah, yeah, I'm coming, I forgive you. Christ, don't have a conniption fit. *(To SAM.)* So, who are you, really? Are you like his agent or something?

SAM. Yes. Something like that.

BUSTER. He also handles the Banana Man.

WAITRESS. Wow. Lucky guy. Well, I gotta go. I had a really nice time on our date, guys. Don't leave until I say goodbye, okay? *(She starts out, comes back, takes off hat, presents it to BUSTER.)* Oh. Here's your hat. *(To the darkness as she goes off again.)* All right, all right, what have you got, an iguana in your shorts?

BUSTER. I am deeply and hopelessly in love with this person.

SAM. As am I.

BUSTER. Let's get the hell out of here before she comes back. I gotta leave this kid a fifty dollar tip.

SAM. I'll chip in.

BUSTER. How much have you got?

SAM. *(Examining the contents of his wallet.)* Forty-nine dollars.

BUSTER. I only need forty-eight. *(SAM looks at him for a moment, then gives him the money.)* Welp. Tomorrow.

SAM. Yes.

BUSTER. When he covers the mirror with the rug?

SAM. Yes?

BUSTER. It's the reflection.

SAM. Yes.

BUSTER. And the parrot, looking at him?

SAM. Yes.

BUSTER. Fish, looking at him.

SAM. Yes.

(Pause.)

BUSTER. I got it.

SAM. Good.

BUSTER. I'll do it good for you.

SAM. I have no doubt.

BUSTER. I'll do it how you want.

SAM. We'll work it out together.

BUSTER. On the off chance that anybody's watching.

SAM. On the off chance.

BUSTER. *(Holds up his bottle.)* To the Banana Man.

SAM. *(Holding up his bottle.)* The Banana Man.

(They clink their bottles together and drink the last of the beer. The light

fades on them and goes out.)

NARRAGANSETT

When Nathaniel Hawthorne and his wife Sophia traveled to Italy in the late 1850s, they took with them as governess for their children Una, Julian and Rose Miss Ada Adaline Shephard of Antioch College, Yellow Springs, Ohio.

After this extended journey, when Miss Shephard's services were no longer required by the Hawthornes, she returned to America to marry her fiancé. Some years later she was drowned off the coast of Narragansett.

(Lights up on ADA, a young American woman, on a boat in Narragansett Bay. The year is 1874. Most of the events she speaks of took place in the late 1850s in Europe.)

ADA

We are just off the coast of Narragansett. I look deep into the cold, black waters. I am not, she said, alas, the celebrated astronomical lady of Nantucket. I am the rain-blurred governess.

In my dreams I still wander the labyrinth of Rome with the Hawthornes. There is beautiful, pale Una, that devil Julian, sweet little Rosebud, tall, brooding Mr Hawthorne, and his dear wife, whose name is synonymous with wisdom. And lurking just there in the corner of the picture, nearly obscured by a tree branch, if you take the trouble to squint, you can barely make out the blurry features of the children's governess, Miss Ada Shepherd. At time of carnival, everybody is a little blurry. We six wander among the harlequins.

Yesterday I saw a large crow in the middle of the road on a rainy morning. There are omens everywhere. The world is made up entirely of omens, if we could only read them. But we have misplaced our spectacles.

The day before we left Rome, Mr Hawthorne took a walk with his pensive daughter Una, and was somewhat taken aback by the intensity of her grief at leaving the city. All daughters are strangers to their fathers, and Rome is a palimpsest of melancholy and desire, rather like Greek pastry. Small bites only, please, Miss Shephard.

Little Rosebud adores Italy. I should not be surprised if one day she did not become a nun. Yes. Una will die young. Rosebud will marry, then become a nun in her widowhood, remembering her happy childhood playing hide and seek with the Pope in the Vatican. The world is God

25

playing hide and seek with himself. And Julian, of course, will end up in prison. I am just a bit psychic, you see. The spirits have informed me over cucumber sandwiches. I can pull ectoplasm out my mouth like taffy. I am one of seven sisters. Look up in the night sky and you can just pick me out. I am the one almost but not quite out of the picture. My face is a little blurred by interstellar nebulosity. I have lived for some years at Antioch, in Yellow Springs. An epistle to the Narragansettians, from Antioch. An epistle to the Nantucketers. Which reminds me of a very moving poem by Henry Wadsworth Longfellow. How does it go?

There once was a girl from Nantucket
Who shut up her soul in a bucket.
She fed it with spiders
And cranberry ciders
And, offering her nipple,
Said, Suck it.

Longfellow stole it from me. No, that's a lie. It was the badger made me say it. The badger follows me everywhere. Longfellow's wife burned to death when the candle caught her dress on fire. Like the willful housecat, nobody could put her out. What a shame she was not floating like Ophelia in Narragansett Bay at the time. Those are pearls that were her eyes.

Mr Hawthorne remembers the picture of the girls gathered about the fallen autumn leaves, the one by Mr Millais he saw in Manchester. We are those four girls. Una and Rosebud and me, and one other who walks always at my side, murmuring in the night. Splash in the dark water. Is somebody missing? Now we must count again.

Mr Hawthorne confesses that he has no natural feeling for art. He's not being modest. It's perfectly true. He met his wife when she came to do his portrait. Sometimes at night I hear her murmuring, and the rhythmic protests of the bed. Oh, God. Oh, God, oh God. In her correspondence, Mrs Hawthorne always spells God with three capital letters, as if she were shouting it out like the town crier. Now I understand the connection. Autumn leaves.

Mr Hawthorne has gone out into the piazza to purchase some cherries. The badger is scratching at the basement window. Narragansett is an Indian word meaning nipples. I love them all to pieces. I love them with

NARRAGANSETT

blood and onions.

Little Rosebud is playing with the children of that sculptor who believes he is God's gift to the horses. I do wish that dribbling satyr would not leer at me so in my dreams. Ada, Ada, you and your six sisters are doomed to be ravished by Greek mythology. Florence is full of nakedness and my love is far away. He has become an entirely imaginary personage. He is yellow pieces of paper with ink stains, like rabbit tracks in the snow. Yellow Springs. Yellow snow. Catacomb bones.

There are seagulls disgracing themselves upon the deck. This, I suppose, is why it's called the poop deck. The seagulls are waiting patiently for me. Birds know. That is why they are birds. They are the souls of the lost, of those that God forgot. I shall become one of them soon. Those are pearls that were my eyes.

Antioch is a place of fallen leaves. When we die, we go to Ohio. Lying naked in the darkness I think of Greek and Roman statues while the clock ticks. I bathe my breasts and Julian peeks at me through the key-hole. Filthy little beast.

Yesterday, a family of five wild turkeys, or turkey vultures, walking about like morose old Italian women or gigantic alien roaches upon the snowy hillside. Narragansett is an Indian word meaning carrion bird.

Una and I have made a midnight excursion to Galileo's tower to observe the constellation Virgo. Her face by starlight makes me want to cry. We walk down a long row of cypresses, surrounded by the murmurings of the dead. I hear something following us, shuffling along in the dust. I wish this gray day out of Goya could last forever. A small vase for holy water, covered in cobwebs.

This morning Mr Hawthorne had difficulty finding his way back to the wooden staircase leading up to the belltower. It is nearly impossible to find the chapel. There are so many rooms, all with brick floors. Cob-webs, unexpected stairways that lead to half floors. The basements are vast. Una goes wandering in them, and Julian enjoys sneaking up on her and blowing on her neck. He knows she is fragile, but he can't seem to help himself. Julian will certainly burn in hell.

NARRAGANSETT

Little Rosebud is playing in the sunshine with her dolly. Grape vines all about. The high wall which circles the estate gives the illusion of safety. We are living in an old Italian painting. I have a nearly overwhelming desire to lie naked in the rank vegetation of the overgrown back garden. This place was a fortress once. Now it is our prison.

And yet the dark Narragansett waters are so cold. I cannot, cannot fathom it. I cannot fathom time, geography or memory. The clock at the center of the labyrinth is a symbol of the union of time and space. It is all rubbish, of course. No symbol means anything. Full fathom five. Shut up. Shut up.

Once, on the open high piazza under the tower, I felt a sudden, powerful impulse to hurl myself down onto the bricks. It was the badger whispering in my ear.

In the chapel next to Una's bedchamber there is an alabaster skull. I can hear it humming in the night like bees. There is a strange and very disconcerting rustling in the weeds. A baby bird? A mouse? Something small and helpless is no doubt being devoured, or having intercourse. Owls haunt the tower. Mother Mary pray for me. Magdalen. Magdalen.

We have been to visit old Mr Kirkup, who has lived in Florence for many years, in a beautiful, dark old palazzo. As a young man he attended the funerals of Keats and Shelley. Mr Edward Trelawny, the drinking companion of Lord Byron, is his oldest friend. All of that was so impossibly long ago, and yet here is Mr Kirkup, like a living ghost, to testify that it was not a dream. Mr Kirkup has a beautiful little dark haired fairy child who greets his guests at the door and gives them a tour of the premises, complete with delightful running commentary. She chatters away most charmingly in English and Italian. Mr Kirkup calls her his child, but Robert Browning says that Imogen is no more Mr Kirkup's daughter than he himself is. I think this rather cruel, but there you are. When the kind are cruel it is somehow uglier than when the cruel are. And yet a careful study of his dramatic monologues reveals that there are many strange and twisted persons lurking inside Mr Browning. He's not the only one.

Mr Kirkup, divining Mr Browning's skepticism about little Imogen's parentage, said, over a crackling fire, Yes, we must doubt everything, but also we must believe everything, and we must do both simultaneously. This I learned from my friend William Blake. In their old age, Blake and his wife used to walk naked in their back garden, holding long conversations with angels.

Let us attempt not to picture that. But the attempt not to picture always fails. Nantucket. Antioch. The copulation of demons.

I have been exercising my faculties as a spirit medium, and my attempts to engage in automatic writing have met with some success, but at night the succubus cometh to knead my flesh. Oh, God, oh, God, oh, God. Squeak, squeak, squeak.

Imogen runs through the castle, very charming, with her little Persian kitten trailing behind her, like a little fairy witch girl and her familiar. Her mother, a lovely young Italian woman of the streets, dead at 19, speaks through me at the seance. Oh, Mr Kirkup, she says. Oh, my darling little Imogen. How I miss you in this strangely familiar land to which I've been exiled. If only I could describe it to you, my dears, but I am forbidden. Do not fear death, she says, but love while you can. It is a great mistake not to love, even not to love foolishly. Her portrait looks at me from the wall. Her dark eyes are fathomless. Her lips were made to kiss. Oh, oh. Copulation. Yellow Springs. Squeak squeak squeak. She was murdered in the room where the orchestra plays when it rains. Lost, lost, lost.

Something has been following us. Something evil. Something wicked this way comes. At night I dream of a huge old badger, creeping down the hillside in the moonlight, towards the house. Help me.

Mr Hume is a great medium. Mr Browning does not like him, and calls him Mr Sludge. He says he is double jointed, and touches people under the table with his bare feet. But I know there is more to Mr Sludge than double joints and long toes. Mr Sludge hovers in the air out the window like a bat.

Ah, yes, my dear, said Mr Sludge, looking at me with his strange transparent eyes. You are one of us. You have the gift. You are fey. You are fey.

NARRAGANSETT

Narragansett, an Indian word meaning horse puckey.

There is mist in the valley of the Arno, and the moon is in the wane. The comet hangs in the sky like a question. It's a message just for me, but it's written in a language in which I am not proficient.

My dreams are haunted by the cries of Florentine fruit vendors. They are selling juicy, dripping peaches. The juice of this peach drips down my chin. All is steaming in the market. The voices and smells, the bodies rubbing together. The people are like ripe fruit.

The Emperor Louis Napoleon is juggling the wooden heads of dolls while the medium, Mr Sludge, is walking about on his hands, and tying up the bow of the Queen of Naples' bonnet with his feet.

The statue of Daniel Webster lies far beneath the ocean, by the transatlantic cable. Those are pearls that were his eyes. The union has not been preserved.

I have a forefinger of Galileo preserved under glass. Dead men's fingers. He used it to pick his nose. If I could remember past lives, I should be so unhappy.

Oh, Mr Hawthorne, what are you doing? And would you like to do it again? Squeak, squeak, squeak.

Enigmatical and tremulous is the sparrow in the hand. Puckery cider apples fallen among the leaves. Who is the girl in the dark Corinthian mirror?

Mr Powers has introduced us to his automatons. They are wax mannikins who move and speak like people, only they are not liars. At night, when the museum is dark, the mannikins are copulating. Squeak, squeak, squeak.

Mr Hawthorne is in love with the Venus de Medici. He longs to be enfolded in her arms. It is a tragic story.

Dead Florentines on the cobbles before the palazzo. Naked, naked, at night when we are gone, the statues copulate in the moonlight. Cold

NARRAGANSETT

Narragansett water. We dwell in the dark of the moon.

The badger observes copulation from the other side of the dirty window pane. I awaken, my heart beating, and there is a cuttle fish on my pillow. A pair of bronze hands are crawling up the counterpane to strangle me. It isn't what happens that kills you. It's what you remember.

Captain Norbert had the finest collection of Narwhal tusks in the world, yet he was not happy.

One day, the shoemaker Jacob Boehme saw the sunlight fall with particular brilliance upon a pewter dish, and suddenly discovered he could see deep, deep into the heart of all things.

Looking at herself in the restaurant mirrors, Miss Shepard realized that she was seeing somebody else entirely.

What does it matter whose child she is? As long as she is loved. She seems to have a happy life. We are all orphans.

Once the chocolate has set, remove the tarts.

I am suffering from a spasm of the glottis.

This gift of automatic writing is a two edged sword. I tell Mr Hawthorne that I believe nothing of it, but in my soul I know better. Mr Hume-Sludge and I have secret knowledge. The other world keeps whispering in my head. It says the water is cold, and yet there are mermaids beckoning. The seagulls are not my friends. They are waiting.

Well, this is a droll melange. We all go to the cathedral in Siena and attempt to draw it, except for Mr Hawthorne, who is trying to write about it, but the cathedral defeats us all. Reality defeats art. All representation is ultimately futile.

I have seen Una's ghost moving through the dark cathedral of Siena, which is all the more remarkable because Una is not dead. I am forever haunted by Gothic oddities. There is a very peculiar man playing the accordion by the river. His teeth are vile. I am the strange visitor.

Standing on the tower, I can see ghostly lights. Cast yourself down, says the badger, whispering in my head.

Mr Hawthorne comes up here to smoke cigars and look at the comet. It is a vice he attempts to hide from Mrs Hawthorne. She knows, of course. She is the pure font of all holiness. How I should enjoy cutting her throat with a shard of broken looking glass and watching the blood stream scarlet down her breasts.

The period of Donati's comet is two thousand years. Thus the comet we observe over Florence in October of the year 1858 would have appeared last in the year 142 BC or thereabouts. It should come again about 3858. I do not expect to see it. Call me a pessimist.

At the height of the comet's grandeur, we all go out at night to gaze upon it and wonder. Mr Hawthorne, Mrs Hawthorne, Una, Julian, Rosebud, and me. They are all one flesh. I am the mad governess. The separateness is unbearable. I want to melt my naked flesh into them forever.

I am the statue of America, bare to the waist. Look at my breasts, I said to the mirror. Something touches them in the night. That little monster Julian is peeking through the keyhole. Let him. The twins suckle at the teats of the great bronze wolf goddess.

I can hear it getting darker, said my father. The night has got into my head.

I wander through the dark palazzo at night. Something touches my breasts.

Julian is throwing a fit because we did not visit the castle of the bandit king. Mr Hawthorne explains that darkness would make the return too dangerous, but Julian is furious and unconsolable. Julian has no interest in consequences. He is only interested in bandits and naked women. Una is very pale. I think the vampire follows us to Rome.

In this place was the Queen strangled in her bath. And here it was that Mr Hawthorne and the others abandoned us. Una and I, having got out to stretch our legs, looked up to discover the coach disappearing down the road, and we two maidens left to the tender mercies of Italy, of which, fortunately, there are some. It was little Rosebud who discovered we were missing and raised the alarm. The adults did not notice at all. Julian saw but said nothing. He is the Devil incarnate.

The Prince of Wales gives Una a bouquet. He looks at her as if he'd like to give her more than that. Filthy creatures. Badger eyes. The creature is closer now.

Something has bitten poor Una upon her breast. It has crept into her bedroom at night to suckle at her flesh. In the morning, she is very pale. The others believe she has caught Roman fever by sitting down to sketch in the Colosseum. She speaks in delirium, often in blank verse, and believes herself to be hovering, like Mr Sludge. Then she is better. Her cheeks are red.

It is Carnival again. Monstrous and grotesque, the snouts of the carnival animals, the snub nosed dog thing and the fierce baboon. An infinite number of clowns. Buckets of confetti are emptied upon us. Young men with the faces of monkeys touch our breasts. Hideous grins and monstrous noses. Beasts everywhere, all in and out of the fog.

The women wear knives in their hair. If a gentleman is rude, it is permissible, at Carnival, to cut off his pizzle, and wear it as a badge upon one's breast.

If you look at it from outside, it depresses you. But if you can get inside it, it possesses you. Now all the tapers are being extinguished, one by one, like the stars at the end of the universe. As the Carnival wanes, so Una is wasting away.

I believe I have seen the one who sucks at her in the night. He has the face of a badger, and his hands are very strong. He has touched me under the counterpane.

When she whimpers in the night, I slip into Una's bed and hold her. She is trembling, her hands and feet are cold. I press her two hands in mine, and tuck my bare feet under the soles of hers. I can feel her pressing against me. For a moment, I wonder what the blood in her neck would taste like. I kiss her there, tenderly. Two red marks, like eyes glowing in the dark. We can hear the last of the revellers going home in the street below. I kiss her lips. She tastes like honey.

Would you like to see photographs of my Puck? Are these bracelets or manacles? Eye of the beholder. Mr Story remarked to me in Siena that he found the expression on the Venus de Medici quite insipid, and that he should like nothing better than to knock her head off. Mr Hawthorne, who loved her once, now is also bored with her. Her naked form does not lure him to her as it did before. These men have the morals of hyenas. They should all be killed.

At night I examine myself in the mirror in my room. But I am spoiled. I am cursed with arms.

They have dug up another Venus at the edge of the city, in the ruins of a bathroom. Her head is off, her fingers lie about her, she is filthy, but oh, how beautiful among the rubbish. The workman puts her head back on for our edification. She has slept long beneath the earth. Oh, my dear, do not be modest. Let them see your mysterious parts. They are not fit to slide their tongues upon your nether lips.

There is so much lurking under the earth. But the digging is painful, and filthy, and one never knows if one will find the statue of Venus, in all her nude glory, or some hideous, putrid, corpse. The man who owns the field where the Venus was found has the most hideous purple face, bloated, with a red swollen nose, a face out of a nightmare, the face of a badger. How disconcerting that he, who is alive, looks as if he's the one who's just been dug up, while she, who has never lived, has been buried under the earth for a thousand years, and yet seems quite as alive as the day some shy Greek girl disrobed and modelled for her. In the midst of life, death, and in the midst of death—

We are walking in the catacombs, deep under Rome, down a broad flight of stone steps, carrying wax tapers, relics of the now dead carnival, through intricate passageways lined with niches full of old skulls and yellow bones. They crumble to dust in my fingers. Ashes. I hear the creature following.

Now and then we come upon little chapels hidden among the dark, creeping, tortuous passages, decorated with faded and grotesque frescoes covered with damp, red and purplish mold. Skeletons gape at us from behind glass. The passages go downwards, upwards, downwards again,

NARRAGANSETT

like a nightmare. Bottles with blood. Long lines of lit tapers before and behind us, the dead coming to find their berths. I have entered a labyrinth constructed entirely of human bones. I am haunted by the faces of dead Etruscans. In the labyrinth of the castle of the false popes of Avignon, blood stains appear on the walls. I have learned to love despair. The fourth step is into darkness. At the bottom of the pit there is a pile of skeletons. I see a hand moving. Skeleton fingers touching. Trying to write in filth upon stone. Lure the creature downwards, then destroy him.

I am awakened in the night by the sound of the window being forced up. In the moonlight I can just make out something large and hairy creeping over the windowsill. My heart is pounding. I dare not move a muscle. The stench of the creature is dreadful, yet oddly exciting. Musk. He has pulled himself up onto the bed. I feel the pressure of him on my thighs, pushing my nightgown up above my breasts. This hideous creature's weight upon me is unbearable. His terrible breath. His snout. Then I feel him entering into me. I want to scream, but my mouth is full of confetti. I think of poor Una. I shall sacrifice myself for Una. I shall give myself up in her place.

I hope that life is like a book we can take down from the shelf in the library of God when we're dead, turn to our favorite passages and read them over from time to time, skipping the parts that fill us with agony, or make us feel ashamed.

I have decided now. I shall become one of the Rhine maidens, naked in the water. Men will gaze upon my lovely corpse and desire the creature I was. We love too soon, we love before we have properly understood the creature we think we love, or we love too late. Everything worth knowing is known too soon, and understood too late.

After Italy, of course, my services were no longer required. But do not be troubled, I said to them. I am engaged to marry Mr Henry Clay Badger of Yellow Springs, Ohio.

I look down into the black Narragansett water. Yes, I think. This is the day. I would not be mad, sweet Jesus. Full fathom five.

I know what I must do, and yet the water is so cold. If only the creature were not clawing at me so, night after night, perhaps I could linger a while. But to linger in madness is vile. Forgive me, Una. Forgive me, little Rosebud. Forgive me, even, you dreadful men, Mr Hawthorne, and Julian, and the thing at the window who crawls upon me to violate me each night. I do this to save you, my love. I do this to redeem us all from the madness of unholy conjugation. Learn from my sacrifice, Una, my dear, and teach your little Rosebud to close like the petals of the orchid at night. Those are pearls that were my eyes.

(A moment. Then, blackout. In darkness, the sound of gulls.)

IDA LUPINO
IN THE DARK

CHARACTERS

MINNIE, a young woman
SHERRY, her younger sister
CAITLIN, her older sister

SETTING

A sofa in a darkened room. An overturned bicycle with horn, an old keyboard, a tape player, a trumpet, a fog horn, a train whistle, various pieces of bizarre junk scattered about.

Ida Lupino (looPEEno) (1918-1995), actress, director, screenwriter, born in London, descended from a celebrated Italian company of players who fled there in the 1600s. A movie star from her teen years, she appeared with Humphrey Bogart in *They Drive By Night* and *High Sierra*, with Ronald Coleman in *The Light That Failed*, with Basil Rathbone and Nigel Bruce in *The Adventures of Sherlock Holmes*, with Jack Palance in *The Big Knife*, with Robert Ryan in *Beware My Lovely*, with John Garfield in *Out of the Fog*, as Emily Bronte in *Devotion*, and in many other films. She began directing in her thirties and for years was the only woman in the Director's Guild. But it was difficult for her to get directing jobs in the male-dominated jungle of Hollywood, and some of her best work was done in television in the 1950s and early 1960s, directing episodes of *The Untouchables* and *The Fugitive*. She also appeared on *The Twilight Zone* and *Columbo*, and had her own show for a while with her husband Howard Duff. She continued to act and direct until her retirement in 1978. In her last film appearance, in a remarkably appropriate mirroring of her experiences in Hollywood, she was attacked by huge worms and finally devoured by gigantic rats.

(A darkened room, lit by an invisible downstage television which casts an eerie glow on MINNIE. The sound is turned way down, and in fact there's just snow on the channel. She is surrounded by a rather odd collection of junk: an upturned bicycle with a horn and a playing card attached by the spokes of one wheel, a tape player, an old keyboard, a trumpet, a gong, various horns and things.)

MINNIE. Sydney Greenstreet sweats under the rotating ceiling fan, sucking on his hookah, while in the twisted labyrinth of Paris, Peter Lorre is being chased by a severed hand. Sam Spade pours himself another Scotch as we flash back to Ingrid Bergman weeping in the gazebo while Cary Grant creeps through the moonlit bedroom window and Paganini's violin wails like a demon lover. *(She pushes a button on the tape recorder and we hear a bit of lush violin movie score.)* Suddenly a huge black raven flaps in the window. CAWWW CAWWW CAWWW. You can hear the film cricketing through the sprockets. *(She turns the music off and rotates the pedal of the upside down bicycle. The Queen of Spades flapping against the spokes makes the sound of an old film projector.)* Boston Blackie lights his cigar, and we see revealed the face of Veronica Lake, but Conrad Veidt is lurking like a preying mantis in the cobbled alleyway. *(She plays a dramatic and ominous organ chord on her keyboard.)* He is a Nazi vampire golem, the zombie servant of Bela Lugosi. Then, in the distance, we hear the sound of a lonely fog horn. *(She turns on her fog horn. A very loud sound.)* It's Spencer Tracy, home from King Solomon's Mines.

(She blows the fog horn again. A door opens upstage, and there's a little shaft of light in the darkness. It's her younger sister SHERRY.)

SHERRY. Minnie? Is everything all right?
MINNIE. Scrub the poop deck, Long John! cries Tugboat Annie. All ashore that's going ashore.

(MINNIE blows the foghorn again. SHERRY jumps.)

SHERRY. Jesus, Minnie, what have you got, the Queen Mary in here?

MINNIE. Close the door. You're letting the dark out.

SHERRY. Letting the dark out? How can I let the dark out?

MINNIE. Just close the goddamned door or I'm going to start screaming like a banshee at a rectal exam.

SHERRY. *(Closing the door.)* All right, all right. God, Minnie, what's the matter with you?

MINNIE. Minnie is only a role I play. She's my nom de plume. Actually I'm Ida Lupino.

SHERRY. Who?

MINNIE. It's New York in the forties, but they've all met before, in Morocco. Bogie has nightmares in which he sees these ceiling fans spinning forever. He got a touch of malaria from Shanghai Lil on the road to Mandalay. Gray rain drips off the brim of Orson Welles' hat, in the sewers under Grand Central Station. *(She blows a horn that makes a loud train whistle sound.)* Quiet, my little babushka. No one can be trusted in Tangiers. There are Nazi spies everywhere. Claude Rains is invisible. There's a microphone hidden in Adolph Menjou's mustache. The Marx Brothers are running through the Grand Hotel, past Buster Keaton, who's sharing a corned beef sandwich with Francis the Talking Mule. *(She honks the bicycle's horn three times.)* They've got to win back the circus for Maureen O'Sullivan in the big horse race at the Bowery.

(She produces a trumpet and blows a loud racetrack fanfare.)

CAITLIN. *(Bursting in the door. We see the stream of light again.)* What the hell is going on in here? It sounds like a marching band exploded.

SHERRY. It's not me. It's Minnie.

MINNIE. I'm not Minnie. Minnie is a mouse with white gloves and three fingers who has occasional intercourse with her consort, Wallace Beery. I'm Ida Lupino.

CAITLIN. You're not Ida Lupino. You're my sister Minnie. Ida Lupino is dead. I think she's dead. Is Ida Lupino dead?

SHERRY. Who is Ida Lupino?

MINNIE. I'm not dead. I'm directing. First you direct. Then you die.

CAITLIN. Directing what?

MINNIE. Would you please shut the door? I'm trying to work in here. Places for the big waterfall number. Virgins on the right.

CAITLIN. And why is it so dark in here?

(CAITLIN turns on the light.)

MINNIE. *(Holding her face like Edvard Munch and commencing a long series of earsplitting screams.)* AHHHHHHH. AHHHHH. AHHHHHH. AHHHHHHH. AHHHHH.

CAITLIN. What's wrong? What's the matter? Honey, what's the matter?

MINNIE. AHHHHHH. AHHHHIIH. AHHHHHH. AHHHHHH. AHHHHHHH.

CAITLIN. Sherry, what did you do to her?

SHERRY. I didn't do anything to her.

CAITLIN. Then why is she screaming?

SHERRY. What?

CAITLIN. I SAID, WHY IS SHE SCREAMING?

MINNIE. AHHHHHHH. AHHHHHHHHH. AHHHHHHHHHH.

SHERRY. She's a banshee at a rectal exam.

CAITLIN. What?

SHERRY. It's the light. Turn off the light.

(She pushes her way past CAITLIN to get to the light switch.)

CAITLIN. Have you two been drinking?

MINNIE. AHHHHHHHHII. AHHHHHHHHH. AHHHHHHHHH. *(SHERRY turns off the lights. MINNIE stops in mid-scream.)* And close the door while you're at it.

SHERRY. Okay. Okay.

(She closes the door.)

CAITLIN. Will somebody tell me what's going on here?

SHERRY. You were letting the dark out.

MINNIE. Quiet on the set. Okay. Roll em.

CAITLIN. Who is she talking to? Is Mac here?

MINNIE. *(Turning the bicycle pedal, making the whirring sound again.)* The fog rolls in over Baker Street.

(She blows the fog horn.)

CAITLIN. *(Nearly jumping out of her skin.)* Will you stop that?

MINNIE. Marlena Dietrich wants to hire Philip Marlowe, who keeps getting phone calls from Erich von Stroheim, who's dead. Ann Sothern is his wise-cracking secretary. Meanwhile, in the dark house in the country, George Brent is trying to drive Merle Oberon insane. He's strangled Rhonda Fleming under the spiral staircase.

SHERRY. Who are these people?

CAITLIN. Something's happened to Minnie. Minnie, what's wrong? What happened?

MINNIE. Boris Karloff is burying ZaSu Pitts in the garden while Lon Chaney fingers his organ in the subterranean catacombs. *(She plays an the ominous organ chord again.)* His son Larry turns to a wolf when the wolfbane blooms, and at the gypsy caravan, Aquanetta has the bumps on her head read by Marya Ouspenskaya, who gazes deep into her crystal monkey and warns her to beware of George Zucco. As the rain falls on Castle Frankenstein, Charlie Chan arrives.

(She hits a gong with a mallet, very loud.)

CAITLIN. *(Holding up skull-shaped bongos.)* What is all this crap?

MINNIE. This is the crap of my husband, Howard Duff, the famous actor. Great Scott, Watson, what a fool I've been! Pray God we may not be too late!

CAITLIN. Your husband isn't Howard. Your husband is Mac. And he's not an actor. He's an artist. Well, he thinks he's an artist.

MINNIE. Howard thinks he's an artist, too. But I'm the artist in the family. I come from a proud European theatrical dynasty.

CAITLIN. Minnie, you come from Ohio.

SHERRY. Mac is a wonderful artist. This must be the stuff he's collecting for his new three dimensional musical collage. He's incredibly inventive.

CAITLIN. Like many criminals before him. Why is there just snow on the television?

MINNIE. That's for atmosphere. I like the ghostly glow. I was deeply influenced by Fritz Lang, Nosferatu and Krazy Kat.

SHERRY. Also they disconnected the cable. Mac was late paying the bill.

CAITLIN. Mac never pays for anything. It's the people around him who pay.

MINNIE. Places for the zebra stampede. Time is money, people. Look, Jungle Jim. It's Sabooo, the Elephant Boy!

(She makes a loud elephant noise with the trumpet.)

CAITLIN. If you don't stop blowing that damned thing I'm going to take it away from you and wrap it around your neck. I mean it, Minnie.

MINNIE. I'm not your stupid sister Minnie. I'm Ida Lupino. I'm the last in a long and illustrious line of Lupinos, which is also, incidentally, a kind of nut.

SHERRY. No kidding.

MINNIE. My ancestors were celebrated acrobats in the courts of Italy when yours were painting their asses blue and flirting with baboons. There are generations of Lupinos in my eyes. Charles the Second gave us his royal thundermug.

CAITLIN. Where is that son of a bitch Mac, anyway? Is it too much to hope she's got his head in a hat box in the closet?

SHERRY. It's not Mac's fault she's crazy. He went to New Jersey to get mannikin parts.

CAITLIN. His wife's sitting here in the dark hallucinating about Ida Lupino and baboon asses and he's in New Jersey looking for mannikin parts? What the hell kind of excuse is that?

SHERRY. He does the best he can, but she just gets to be too much for him.

CAITLIN. Why are you always apologizing for that selfish bastard?

SHERRY. Why are you always making excuses for Minnie? You've been doing it since we were little girls. Look at her. She doesn't need excuses. She needs help.

MINNIE. What I need a glockenspiel. And tap shoes. Mother was the fastest tap dancer in England. That's how I got my big break. She was up for a movie but the director took one look at me and they made me dress like Jean Harlow till I was eighteen, then I washed the blonde out and told them they could shove Jean Harlow up Mr DeMille's ass and started my own production company, but on the first day of shooting, the director dropped dead, so I kept the camera rolling and did it myself. And I realized, wow, I'm good at this.

CAITLIN. Honey, you're not a director.

MINNIE. That's what Darryl F. Zanuck told me. He thought men wouldn't take orders from women, at least not in public, but I just say Do Mama a favor, and touch their chest and look soulfully into their eyes, and they'll roll over and bark for me if I want them to. Actors are babies with over-developed gonads. This is the secret of my success.

CAITLIN. Honey, listen, you're upset because your no good worthless pig of a husband has run off again, and you're having a small nervous breakdown.

MINNIE. I don't have nervous breakdowns. I have extremely calm breakdowns. I'm a very strong woman. Howard says so. He really admires me. He especially likes the way my breasts float in the bubble bath when I'm reading Emily Bronte with my little half glasses on and a Margarita in the soap dish.

CAITLIN. Minnie, try and focus here for a second, could you?

MINNIE. Fire in the hole!

(She blows the fog horn.)

CAITLIN. Your husband's name is Mac. He's an idiot, but he's real. You're just a little hysterical.

MINNIE. That's what they always say when a woman tries to direct. But I'm tired of taking direction. I don't want to be clay in somebody else's hands. I want to shape the movie myself. Now get in your places, or I'm kicking some movie star butt around here.

SHERRY. Honey, there's something seriously wrong with you.

MINNIE. Do you want to know the plot of this movie, Sherry?

SHERRY. Not really, no.

MINNIE. Priscilla Lane has two sisters, Olivia de Havilland and Deanna Durbin. And the older sister loves her but she's always trying to protect her so much she's smothering her to death and driving her nuts, while the younger sister's merely sleeping with Priscilla's husband, who's an artist. There really is something seriously wrong with HER. What's wrong is that while she pretends to be all concerned for her sister, in fact she's an evil, conniving little backstabbing bitch. Doesn't that sound like a swell idea for a movie, Sher? *(She looks at SHERRY. SHERRY looks away. CAITLIN looks at SHERRY.)* They wanted me to play the betrayed sister, but I decided to direct instead. Places.

CAITLIN. Sherry, what did you do?

SHERRY. Nothing.

CAITLIN. Sherry.

MINNIE. Places. *(She pats the cushion beside her on the couch.)* Do you want to be in this damned movie or not?

SHERRY. Okay.

(She sits down timidly beside MINNIE.)

MINNIE. See how good I am at giving direction? So THIS is the elephants' burial ground!

(She blows the trumpet in SHERRY'S ear.)

CAITLIN. Sherry, did you do this to her?

MINNIE. Quiet on the set.

SHERRY. Just sit down and be in her movie, all right?

CAITLIN. You did this. You did this to her.

SHERRY. Please, just be in her movie. It's what she wants. It'll make her happy. Please?

MINNIE. Places for the Ziegfield Girls. Move it or take it on the road, honey. *(CAITLIN sits down on the other side of MINNIE.)* Ida, an innocent young girl, is off to find her destiny at the fruitcake factory. But in the shadows of the Hollywood sign, a stranger waits with a black bag and a long knife. Ready? Action. *(She whirrs the bicycle wheel. To SHERRY:)* It's your line, sweetheart.

SHERRY. Uh, well, here I am, off to the fruitcake factory, to find my destiny.

MINNIE. Come on. More feeling. I want more.

SHERRY. Uh, what's that dark man I see, there in the shadows of the Hollywood sign?

MINNIE. *(Turning the bicycle wheel harder.)* More. Don't hold back. Give me everything you've got.

SHERRY. Is that a black bag I see? Is that a knife in his hand?

MINNIE. The fog begins to roll in off the Thames, creeping with catlike stealth down Sunset Boulevard and slowly enveloping the three frightened sisters. One of them is a murderess. One of them is doomed. And one can only watch helplessly as the hands of the clock move inexorably towards midnight, when gigantic worms and humongous rats will come to devour them. Suddenly, without warning, they are all engulfed in impenetrable and hideous yet strangely comforting darkness. Cue the foghorn.

IDA LUPINO IN THE DARK

(CAITLIN blows the fog horn. Blackout.)

BALLOON RAT

for Johanna

(ANNA, a young woman of 30, speaks from a circle of light on an otherwise dark stage.)

ANNA

It was not long before my thirtieth birthday
when I observed the first traces of
the presence of the balloon rat.
It was night in Munich, and the floor
was covered with sagging balloons
left over from my daughter's birthday party,
and, half between sleep and waking,
I gradually became aware
that some of these balloons
were rustling just a bit, moving
oddly upon the floor,
as if they were quietly parting
for something unseen
as it made its way
through the crowd.
Well, that's very odd, I said to myself.
There is something on the floor,
scurrying through the little sea
of shyly hovering balloons.
What on earth could that be?
It's not the cat, for the cat
is sleeping on my feet.
Wake up, cat, I said,
wiggling my toes under her,
I believe this is your area.
This is what we pay you for.
But the cat did not seem too interested
in chasing rats about the room

BALLOON RAT

at four o'clock in the morning.
And when I turned the light on
there was nothing but balloons,
huddled together like mourners
in a little herd by the bookshelves.
If these balloons knew anything
they clearly weren't telling—
too frightened to speak, perhaps.
And scuttling across my brain
like little rat-claw feet
was the ghostly half-remembrance
that all this had happened before.
But then it was gone.
And the rat was gone.
And I couldn't get back to sleep.
But I did observe
in the days just after this,
that the cat did not appear to be
entirely unaware of the balloon rat.
I could see her watching for it,
and now and then her eyes
would fix on some dark corner
and her slightly cross-eyed,
vaguely demented gaze
would come to rest
on the sad little congregation
of slowly sagging balloons.
And then she would look at me
as if she were trying to formulate
a particularly complex question,
or transmit some message of warning.
It was also about this time
that I began to notice
a number of other odd things
about my apartment.
When I dropped a carton of milk one day,
the milk rolled downhill.
I thought this was very odd,
for I couldn't recall observing
such a pronounced slant

BALLOON RAT

in my apartment before.
And yet I could almost
but not quite remember
another time when milk was spilled
and rolled down the old linoleum
in much the same fashion.
Who was it? When was it?
And who was I then?
I couldn't say. But I also noticed that
the windows seemed unusually hard
to get up and down, as if
the dimensions of the frames
had altered slightly, somehow,
gone just a bit askew, like
the windows of Dr Caligari's
cabinet. It was very odd.
And when I lay naked in my bath
at the end of the day,
the candles would flicker,
as if something were passing by
in the darkness just beyond
my little circle of light.
I began to feel more and more
that something was watching me.
When I looked at myself in the mirror
I could feel its beady rodent gaze upon me,
and just out the corner of my eye
I could almost catch a glimpse
of something just behind me.
But when I turned
to look at the thing directly,
there was nothing.
I decided I must take action.
I would trap the thing, but humanely.
So I put out an old shoe box
with a bit of cheese inside,
and propped up the lid with
an old screwdriver.
It was a well-tested cartoon strategy:
the rat smells the cheese,

BALLOON RAT

crawls into the box,
knocks over the screwdriver,
the lid falls, klunk,
and the monster is trapped.
Well, it seemed like a good plan
at four o'clock in the morning.
And just about dawn
while I was dreaming of crayfish
and something nibbling gently at my breasts,
I was awakened by the sound
of the lid falling, klunk.
My heart pounding,
I stumbled into the kitchen
wearing only a tee shirt and socks,
and there was the box, lid closed.
Slowly I crept towards what
I believed was the balloon rat's
cheesy tomb.
Closer and closer.
But then I hesitated.
Now that I had it,
what was I going to do with it?
The whole idea of picking up the box
made me uneasy.
The weight of the rat, shifting
in the box, would be very disturbing,
for some reason.
But I forced myself to reach out
with both my hands
and lift up the box from the floor.
It was suspiciously light.
I shook it gently back and forth.
Something was rattling in there.
I took the lid off the box,
and there was the screwdriver,
and just a crumb or two of cheese.
And suddenly I was certain
that something was watching me
from behind my back.
A chill ran up my spine

BALLOON RAT

and I whirled around to look,
and saw there in the doorway,
clutching her small, stuffed dog,
my little girl, her eyes
big with amusement,
giggling at me.
She thinks this is very funny.
For her it's a kind of cartoon moment.
I am to her the German Daffy Duck.
In the afternoon she watches
cartoons in which a small dog
is searching the world in a vain attempt
to locate his lost fart.
Stinky, cries the cartoon dog,
mourning for his lost flatulence.
Stinky, cries my daughter.
And I do feel a bit cartoony.
For a woman of nearly thirty
to become so obsessed with a rodent
is more than a little foolish.
I should put out spring traps, or poison.
But I hesitate to do this.
I have a child. I have a cat.
I don't like poison. And somehow,
it seems unsportsmanlike.
But I grow more troubled each day.
And I begin to suspect more and more
that the cat is in fact a traitor.
She lets the creature
drink milk from her bowl.
Sometimes I have this feeling
they drink there side by side
when I'm not looking.
The two are conspiring against me.
I stay up all night waiting in the dark,
my daughter's plastic hammer in my hand.
I don't know that I want
to kill the balloon rat exactly.
I just want to whack it over the head
so I'll be able to know it's real.

BALLOON RAT

And the thought of this encounter
fills me with such a strange
mixture of dread and excitement
it's almost erotic.
After a bit I doze off
and dream of something scuttling
down a long, shadowed corridor,
and a rhythmic squeaking noise
in a darkly familiar hotel.
Then I am jolted awake
by the sound of someone crying out
in the street. I can't tell if this person
was laughing, or sobbing, or
if these were cries of ecstasy.
I'm trembling. I decide I need
a cup of tea, to fortify myself,
so I get up and make my way
in the dark to the kitchen,
and as soon as I turn the corner,
I see two red eyes staring at me
from across the room, in the darkness.
I stare at the eyes. The eyes stare at me.
It is time, I think, that we two meet.
Slowly I move towards the eyes,
the plastic hammer clutched in my hand.
My heart is pounding. Every nerve is tingling.
And the kitchen smells so good.
It smells like my childhood.
Warm and safe and good,
like something baking at
my grandfather's hotel.
But the two red eyes don't move.
They do not wink. They do not blink.
I reach out my trembling hand
and turn on the light.
For just a moment I'm blinded.
Then I realize, the two red eyes
are the indicator lights on the oven.
I've forgotten the baked potato
I put in there before I fell asleep.

BALLOON RAT

I hear tittering behind the wastebasket.
The balloon rat is laughing at me.
I need to get out of the house.
So on a rainy Munich afternoon
I take my daughter to visit
the Karl Valentin museum
where strange objects hang on the walls,
visual jokes, three dimensional puns,
familiar things made strange,
fragments from another world,
odd recorded voices whispering at me
from scratchy old recordings,
like the personages of a smokey dream,
and where I am served a revolting white sausage
by a girl with a mustache
while across the room a mechanical woman
is touching herself and laughing at me.
And just for a moment
I think I can see in her eyes
the eyes of the balloon rat
looking out at me.
And I remember,
like the fragment of a dream,
another time in which
I was lying in bed with my lover,
a person now far across the ocean,
happy and naked there in the dark,
cuddled together like newborn babies,
when from across the room in the dark
I heard the sound of something
scuttling among fallen balloons.
I like this place, said my little girl,
breaking the spell,
but I don't like these white sausages.
The mechanical woman laughs,
and we walk home in the rain,
up the dark staircase,
the building smells of time and damp
and centuries of sadness and regret,
and as I am fumbling for my keys

BALLOON RAT

I think I can hear something
rustling on the other side of the door.
I tell my daughter to stand back.
Then I raise up my closed umbrella,
ready to strike, take a deep breath,
turn the knob and open the door
to meet my destiny.
The door creaks.
Darkness inside,
the smell of peppermints,
and the ticking of my grandfather's old clock.
Then I hear it again, something rustling
there in the darkness.
I clutch the umbrella tighter
and turn on the light.
SURRRPPPPRRRISE!!!!!!
everybody screams.
The umbrella opens.
I drop it on my foot
and fall backwards
into the coat rack.
It's a birthday party.
They've all been waiting in the dark.
My daughter looks very pleased with herself.
She knew and kept the secret.
My friends think my entrance
was very funny, like Karl Valentin.
And all night long
they do imitations of
me brandishing my umbrella
as the light comes on
and it opens and falls,
and we all have a rather good time.
When the last of them is gone,
I am feeling much better, and yet
also rather empty. I'm very tired.
There is one piece of birthday cake left.
I start to put it in the refrigerator,
and then I stop. I decide
to leave it out for the balloon rat.

BALLOON RAT

I don't know why. Perhaps
a kind of peace offering.
Perhaps the creature is lonely.
Then I go to bed and dream
a series of weird, distorted
interlocking dreams of a sinister
yet familiar house in the woods.
The house is like a labyrinth.
I wander through it,
looking for somebody.
I don't know who.
Someone I used to know,
or used to be.
The answer always seems to be
just around the next corner.
I don't know what it is.
But I know it's all happened before,
like a play I saw in another life.
I don't know what will happen next,
but I know that as it happens
I'll be remembering it.
I can hear the mechanical woman
laughing in another room.
I reach out for someone warm beside me
and discover that somehow
all the balloons
have made their way into my bed
and are nestled there like baby birds.
When I wake up, it's morning.
Birds sing out my window.
The world is still and perfect.
I feel as if I've been asleep
for a thousand years,
like a princess in a fairy tale.
But I can't remember
who kissed me awake.
I get up and go in to say
good morning to my daughter.
Mama, she says, how soon
will it be my birthday again?

BALLOON RAT

Too soon, I say, and
kiss her on the head.
Then I go out to the kitchen
to make some coffee
and look at the table.
Something has eaten the piece of cake,
all except one little perfect rose
made out of icing, which appears
to have been carefully arranged
right in the center of the plate.
The balloon rat has left me a rose.
I am very pleased.

(The light fades on her and goes out.)

BAREFOOT
IN NIGHTGOWN
BY CANDLELIGHT

Barefoot In Nightgown By Candlelight was first produced in September of 2001 by Shadowbox Cabaret in Columbus, Ohio with the following cast:

ALICIA	Pam Callahan
BELLE	Jennifer Hahn
CATH	Colleen Dalton

It was directed by Steve Guyer.

The play was also produced in September of 2001 by the Grey Wing Stage Company in New York City, directed by Larissa Lowe.

CHARACTERS

ALICIA
BELLE
CATH

SETTING

A dim circle of light on an otherwise bare stage, where three young girls in nightgowns huddle together and speak. The feeling of candlelight should be created, but there should be no actual candles.

An important note on safety:
Candles and nightgowns are dangerous together, especially onstage. There should be no actual lit candles in any production of this play.

(Lights up on three young girls, barefoot, in white nightgowns, by candlelight, surrounded by darkness.)

CATH
Do you want to play the game, she said?
My life is this tale told: an orphan girl
sent to Miss Evesham's boarding school in the country
by distant relations who want my inheritance
but not me. Glimpse of a dark old house
nearly strangled by vines and a labyrinth
of overgrown hedges. Very lonely at first.
But then one night I was awakened by
another girl blowing gently upon my face.

ALICIA
Come with me. Don't make a sound
or Miss Evesham will hear.

CATH
Barefoot, in nightgown, by candlelight
she leads me by the hand up a maze
of dark stairways to an attic room.
The door closes behind me.
In a corner of the attic hidden by
some old trunks, another girl waits.

ALICIA
You may speak now, but softly.

CATH
We're not supposed to be here.
We're supposed to be in bed.

BAREFOOT IN NIGHTGOWN BY CANDLELIGHT

If Miss Evesham catches us —

BELLE
She'll beat us. She'll strip off our nightgowns,
tie our hands together, hang us from
the crossbeams and whip our flesh
until we bleed.

CATH
Why did you bring me here?

ALICIA
We've chosen you.

CATH
Chosen me for what?

ALICIA
To be the third member.

BELLE
We must have three.

ALICIA
Three is a magic number.

CATH
The third member of what?

BELLE
We must swear you to secrecy first.

ALICIA
On pain of death.

BELLE
Do you swear never to tell a soul what we do here?

CATH
I don't believe in swearing.

BAREFOOT IN NIGHTGOWN BY CANDLELIGHT

ALICIA
You must swear, or we can't tell you.

CATH
Oh, all right. I swear.

BELLE
On pain of death?

CATH
I swear on pain of death. What is this?

ALICIA
This is the game of Mistress and Slave.
We shuffle this pack of cards
and deal them out to each of us
until one gets the Queen of Spades or Hearts
and then to the other two until
one gets the other Queen, Hearts or Spades.
The Queen of Spades demands one act
from the Queen of Hearts. Just one.
But it may be anything. And the Queen of Hearts
must do it, no matter what it is.

CATH
But what if she doesn't want to?

ALICIA
It doesn't matter what she wants.
She is the Slave. She must.

CATH
But what if she doesn't?

ALICIA
She must.

BELLE
She must.

ALICIA
So. Do you wish to play?

CATH
I might have stopped it here,
before it had properly begun.
But I was afraid, and curious, and lonely.
And here were the two most brilliant
and most beautiful girls in the school
inviting me to join them in
their very secret, very exclusive game.

ALICIA
Cath, do you wish to play the game?

CATH
Yes. I wish to play the game.

ALICIA
Then shuffle the cards and deal.

CATH
Belle gets the Queen of Spades.
I get the Queen of Hearts.

ALICIA
Belle is the Mistress. Cath is the slave.
I am the Witness. Now you must say,
Mistress, what is your desire?

CATH
Mistress, what is your desire?

BELLE
My desire is that you should kiss me, Slave.

CATH
Kiss you?

BAREFOOT IN NIGHTGOWN BY CANDLELIGHT

BELLE
Kiss me, long and tenderly, lips to lips.

CATH
But I've never, I mean, that's not—

ALICIA
Do you wish to play the game or not?

CATH
Yes. I wish to play the game.
And so I kiss Belle, long and tenderly,
lips to lips, barefoot, in nightgown,
by candlelight. She is very beautiful.
And there is something wild and tender
and dangerous in her eyes. After the kiss
she touches my cheek. I'm blushing fiercely and
my heart is pounding like a drum.
Now you are one of us, she says.

ALICIA
Now you are one of us.

CATH
Once a month, at full moon, do we three
creep to the attic at midnight, to play the game,
Alicia, Belle, and me, barefoot,
in nightgown, by candlelight.
Part of the joy of the game, I find,
is its secrecy, its forbidden nature,
the element of chance, the two Queens
lurking somewhere in the pack of cards,
the almost unbearable anticipation
from one full moon to the next,
and being completely at the mercy of
another girl. And being watched
by a third. The danger. It is the danger.

ALICIA
Mistress, what is your desire?

BAREFOOT IN NIGHTGOWN BY CANDLELIGHT

BELLE
Go down to the parlor, Slave,
and dance naked before the fire.

CATH
Down the steps we creep, barefoot,
in nightgown, by candlelight, to the parlor,
my heart pounding violently in fear
and anticipation. Belle and I sit and watch
as Alicia removes her nightgown and stands naked
and shivering by the fire. Then she begins
to dance very solemnly before us,
the firelight glowing upon her naked flesh.

BELLE
Cath holds my hand tightly as we watch
the naked girl, dancing in firelight.
I put her hand just above my left breast.
Feel my heart pounding, I say.
I put my hand on her heart.

CATH
These are the flames of Hell, I think,
and they are very beautiful.

BELLE
We feel each other's blood race through our bodies.
Alicia looks at us as she dances. Is she
jealous, perhaps? How nice if she would be.

CATH
Mistress, what is your desire?

ALICIA
Steal something from Miss Evesham's night stand
by her bed while she sleeps.

BELLE
We creep down the staircase, barefoot,

BAREFOOT IN NIGHTGOWN BY CANDLELIGHT

in nightgown, by candlelight, to Miss Evesham's room,
breathless. Cath opens the door. It creaks.
We glide like ghosts to her bed. I shield the candle
with my hand, feeling its heat on my flesh.

ALICIA
I don't know what's more thrilling: being the Mistress,
the Slave, or the Witness, or the changing of roles
from moon to moon. But watching is very exciting.

CATH
Miss Evesham lies sleeping, breathing softly,
clutching her pillow. On the stand by her bed
is a photograph of a young man. I reach out
my hand towards it, grasp it, clutch it between my breasts,
and back away into the darkness.

BELLE
Mistress, what is your desire?

ALICIA
Crawl out onto the roof, Slave, and walk
to the very edge, and look down, and then count
to a hundred before you return.

CATH
Alicia, Belle is deathly afraid of heights.
She told us so.

ALICIA
I know what she told us.

CATH
Give her something else to do.

ALICIA
The function of the Witness in this game
is to watch. The Witness must not interfere.
I am the Mistress, she is the Slave. She must
do whatever I desire. Belle?

BAREFOOT IN NIGHTGOWN BY CANDLELIGHT

BELLE
Yes?

ALICIA
Crawl out onto the roof, Slave, and walk
to the very edge, and look down, and count
to a hundred. Belle? Do you want to play the game?

BELLE
Yes. I want to play the game.

CATH
The old house has many half-floors and sub-attics.
The roofs are old and crazy quilted, with odd gables,
and steeply slanted. We make our way, barefoot,
in nightgown, by candlelight, to the gable window
at the very top. You don't have to, Belle, I say.

BELLE
I am the Slave. I want to play the game.

CATH
We watch her climb out the window and make her way
down the steep roof, under a blueblack sky,
a full moon and Venus, blue and cold, looking on.
When she reaches the edge she totters. A piece of slate
rolls down the roof and into the air, and smashes
on the cobbles of the courtyard far below.
She steadies herself, looks down, and begins to count.

BELLE
One. Two. Three. Four. Five. Six.

CATH
Let her come in. Let her come in now, Alicia.
She'll get dizzy and fall. She'll kill herself.

ALICIA
If we startle her now, she'll fall. If we interfere,

she'll fall. She must be allowed to play the game.

CATH
She counts, balanced there at the edge
of the roof, under the full moon. It seems
to go on forever. Tears roll down my face.
Alicia is trembling. We hold hands and watch.
Belle sways a bit. We are very excited.

BELLE
Ninety-eight. Ninety-nine. A hundred.

CATH
Then there is a pause. Belle doesn't move.

ALICIA
You can come in now, Slave. Come away from the edge.
Belle, your Mistress desires you to come back in.

BELLE
You've already had your desire. You mustn't be greedy.

CATH
Alicia begins to sob.

ALICIA
Please. Belle, please.

CATH
She is sobbing her heart out. Everything is still.
And then, very calmly, with great assurance, Belle
makes her way back up the roof and in the window.
Alicia holds her and sobs. Belle comforts her.

BELLE
It's all right. I'm all right.

CATH
That was cruel. That was horribly, horribly cruel.

BELLE
It was the game.

CATH
You could have been killed.

BELLE
That's the game.

CATH
Mistress, what is your desire?

BELLE
Go to the piano room at night, Slave,
and kill Miss Evesham's canary.

CATH
I don't want to kill a canary. I don't think
we should be killing things.

BELLE
It's just a bird.

CATH
It's a living creature.

ALICIA
So was the chicken you had for dinner. Would
you feel better about killing the canary
if she'd let you eat it after?

CATH
That's disgusting. Why can't we just be friends?
Why must we do these things? It's gone too far.
I don't like this game any more.

ALICIA
You've chosen to play, and once you're in the game,
you're in the game. Either you're one of us,
or you're not.

BAREFOOT IN NIGHTGOWN BY CANDLELIGHT

CATH
Hasn't anybody ever quit playing this game?

ALICIA
One girl did. The girl just before you quit.

CATH
Which girl? Who was it?

ALICIA
You don't know her. She died before you came.

CATH
She died?

ALICIA
Yes. It was very sad.

CATH
How did she die?

ALICIA
Unexpectedly.
      (Pause.)
So. Do you wish to play the game, or not?

CATH
I wish to play the game.

ALICIA
Then go into the piano room and strangle
Miss Evesham's canary.

CATH
We make our way downstairs, barefoot,
in nightgown, by candlelight, to the piano room.
I reach into the cage. I can feel the warm little creature
trembling in my hand. I am crying. I squeeze
my fist until the little neck breaks. Then I go

and open the window and vomit into the flowers.

BELLE
In the morning, when she finds her bird dead, Miss Evesham
is griefstricken and furious. She calls us
all before her and demands to know
who is responsible. No one says anything.

CATH
At night I dream of the helpless little creature,
nestled in the palm of my hand, awaiting its
destruction. Then I dream that I'm that creature.

ALICIA
Mistress, what is your desire?

CATH
Go to the barn, barefoot, in nightgown, by candlelight,
to the pallet where the gardener's one-eyed son
sleeps, and give yourself to him.

ALICIA
Give myself to him? To that filthy boy?

CATH
Do you not wish to play the game?

ALICIA
This is revenge. This is revenge for the canary.

CATH
The canary was Belle's idea.

ALICIA
But I'm the one who made you. I'm the one
you're angry at, the one you're jealous of.

CATH
Do you wish to play the game or not?

BAREFOOT IN NIGHTGOWN BY CANDLELIGHT

ALICIA
Yes. I wish to play the game.

BELLE
We make our way, barefoot, in nightgown,
by candlelight, down the main staircase,
through the kitchen, out into the garden,
through the wild, rank hedges to the barn
where the gardener's one-eyed son sleeps
on his pallet in the hay.

ALICIA
He is not so bad looking, really, despite the one
dead eye, and the dirty clothing. He is not
an altogether unattractive boy.

CATH
When she kneels beside him, the boy wakes up. She touches
his mouth with her fingers. He stares at her with his one
good eye, which is very blue, a robin's egg blue.
Belle and I watch from behind a bale of hay.

BELLE
Alicia slips off her nightgown and stands naked
before the boy. He is trembling. He must think
he's dreaming. Then she pulls the blanket off him,
so we can see him naked, and lies down
on top of him, kissing and caressing him.

CATH
Belle and I cling to each other, hypnotized,
as we watch the boy push her over onto her back
and enter her there in the straw. His excitement is
horrible and obscene, but we can't look away.
Alicia clutches onto him and looks at us.
Her eyes are locked on Belle's eyes, then on mine,
We are trembling. We are horrified, watching this
beastly thing happen there in the straw. I want
to cry out. I can't breathe. I can't see. I am lost.

BAREFOOT IN NIGHTGOWN BY CANDLELIGHT

BELLE
Four weeks later, Miss Evesham finds the photograph
we stole under the mattress of Cath's bed.
She announces in front of the whole school that Cath is
a dirty little thief and the person who
has murdered her canary. Alicia and I
watch as Miss Evesham strikes her in the face
and tells her she will be sent home in the morning.
That night is the night of full moon.

ALICIA
We must play the game one more time.

CATH
What's the point?

ALICIA
We must play the game.

CATH
Your game has ruined my life and lost you your
virginity to an idiot boy and all
our innocence is lost. The game is over.

ALICIA
No. One last time. We must play the game
one last time. Please. If you love me. Please.

BELLE
I think we should play the game.

ALICIA
Do you wish to play the game, or don't you, Cath?
Either one plays, or one doesn't. If you wish
to play the game, then shuffle the cards and deal.

CATH
I look at them. Then I shuffle the cards and deal.

BAREFOOT IN NIGHTGOWN BY CANDLELIGHT

BELLE
Mistress, what do you desire?

ALICIA
Burn up Miss Evesham in her bed.

CATH
She can't burn up—

ALICIA
Shut up, Witness. Your function is to watch,
not to complain. My desire, Slave, is for you
to burn up Miss Evesham in her bed.
Do you wish to play the game?

(Pause.)

BELLE
I wish to play the game.

CATH
And so we creep down the steps, barefoot,
in nightgown, by candlelight, to Miss Evesham's room,
the three of us, Alicia, Belle and I,
and stand by her bed, looking down at her.

BELLE
She looks so peaceful, sleeping there, I think.
I hesitate for just a moment. Then
I remember the look of hatred on her face
when she hit Cath in front of everyone,
and called her those horrible things.
Then I drop the candle on the bed.

CATH
Then everything's burning. The bedclothes are burning,
Miss Evesham's burning, the curtains are burning,
and we three are running down the stairs,
and through the parlor, and out into the garden,
running until we've got to the top of the hill,

and when we turn then to look back it's like a picture
of Hell from Hieronymus Bosch, the house is burning,
everything is burning. They're dead. They're all dead.
They're all burned up in their beds.

    ALICIA
Yes.

    CATH
They're all dead but us.

    ALICIA
Yes.

    CATH
It's horrible. What we've done is horrible.

    BELLE
We've played the game, is all.

    ALICIA
We've played the game. Don't you want
to play the game?

    CATH
We three girls stand on a hill, holding each other
and watching an old house burn. Yes, I say. Yes.
I want to play the game.

    (The light fades on them and goes out.)

WILD TURKEYS

(Lights up on MIRANDA Tully, age 16, sitting in her own circle of light on an otherwise dark stage, wearing a tee shirt and panties, in the morning.)

MIRANDA

They stood in the yard by the woods again this morning.
Seven wild turkeys, shambling along
like spectral old ladies with buzzardy eyes.
They come in the fog and stalk up the hillside
and through the trees, plodding, phlegmatic,
keeping together, mumbling to one another
like mourners at a funeral. They're taller
than I thought they'd be, and more strange.
I don't know where they come from.
They come more often now on foggy mornings,
They seem very pre-occupied, as if
they're waiting for something.
I don't know what it is.
What are they thinking about?
I get up early in tee shirt and panties to vomit,
then have a glass of apple juice,
and find myself drawn compulsively to the window.
I pull back the the curtain and peer out,
and there they are, as I knew they'd be.
I stand by the window and stare at them.
My bare feet and legs are cold,
but I can't seem to turn away.
They're not looking in my direction,
but they know I'm here.
Am I the reason they've come?
The wild turkeys mill about in the fog
as if one of them's lost his pocket watch.

WILD TURKEYS

I want to go outside. I don't care that it's cold.
I want to go up the hill and talk to them.
But something makes me hesitate.
The first one I saw, some days ago,
was a smaller one, wandering alone out there.
It seemed to be lost. I was concerned.
I walked up the hill, right towards it.
I expected the thing to scurry up into the woods,
but the creature just looked at me.
No fear. No anger. Not curiosity, quite.
Perhaps just a hint of expectation.
It looked at me for the longest time,
and I looked back. And then, for the first time,
I felt something moving inside me.
Then the monster turned, as if dismissing me,
or deciding with mild regret that I
had nothing much to offer him that day,
and made its way deliberately through the bushes
and up the ravaged hillside. No rush.
One clawfoot step and then another. Such
ugly feet and beak, such a hideous red thing
hanging down like a stream of blood.
And yet a kind of awkward, eerie, ancient
hideous beauty there.
Lately, more and more, I have been feeling
this nearly overpowering compulsion
to go outside and find out what they want.
Do they want me to follow them?
Is that why they've come?
Is there something they want me to do, or see?
Or understand? Or have the creatures come
for what's inside me? If I followed them
up into the labyrinth of fallen woods,
where would they take me? What
would they do with me? Would they claw
between my legs? Last night I think I dreamed
of a clearing near the top of the wooded hillside
strewn with fallen trees and the bones of others
they've lured there. And in what I think
must be the lingering memory of this dream

WILD TURKEYS

I can see the wild turkeys standing over
a little corpse in the weeds.
The eyesockets of the little thing are empty,
the bones of the ribcage picked quite clean.
The turkeys stand around the wretched lost
child-thing's remains and look at me.
And I look in their eyes and suddenly
I know what they're trying to say to me.
Make a wish, they say.
On behalf of the darkly wattled gobbling
black carniverous god
of all the wild turkeys of the noble
ancient dying east Ohio woods,
we, the ushers of this place,
invite you to make a wish.
You can't have her, I say, clutching
my stomach with both hands under my shirt.
You can't have her.
She's mine. She's mine.

*(MIRANDA sits there, touching her stomach tenderly under her tee shirt
   with the palms of her hands. The light fades on her and goes out.)*

THE TALE
OF THE
JOHNSON BOYS

The Tale Of The Johnson Boys was first produced by the Grey Wing Stage Company in New York City in September, 2001, directed by Larissa Lowe.

CHARACTERS

John
Henry

SETTING

Late 1790s, near the Ohio River. Night. A flickering light like a fire from down center, just revealing the faces and hands, and, dimly, the rest of the two boys, who are in their late teens at the time of this telling. The events they speak of happened a few years earlier. All the rest of the stage is in darkness.

John Huff (1775-1842) son of Michael Huff Junior and Hannah Doddridge, married Sarah Ann (Sally) Johnson on July 3rd, 1798, five years after the adventure her brothers John and Henry had with the Indians. John Johnson was thirteen in 1793, and his brother Henry was eleven. They lived on the Virginia side of the Ohio, not far above what was then called Indian Short Creek, in what's now the West Virginia Panhandle. My grandmother's grandmother was a Huff cousin of these Huffs, and the story has survived for two hundred years.

(JOHN and HENRY, two boys in their late teens, sit staring into the down center fire, surrounded by darkness.)

JOHN. We had got pretty far into the woods, farther than we was supposed to, and we sat down on a log so Henry could rest, and got interested in the ants in the log, and I looked up and saw two men walking towards us. The sun was in my eyes, blinding me pretty good, and I thought at first it was the Huffs coming home from hunting. It wasn't till they was nearly on top of us that I realized they was two Indians.

HENRY. The Huffs was always out sneakin up on us for fun. They was good at that, although they was both big as buffaloes.

JOHN. I yelled for Henry to run, but he thought I was horsing around, which we'd been doing some, and pulled in the other direction.

HENRY. We was playing Indians. I didn't know it was real.

JOHN. I could have run off and left him, but I didn't. He was my little brother. He was eleven. I kept trying to pull at him until the Indians was on us and then it was too late and they had us both.

HENRY. I was scared. We was playing and then all of a sudden it was real, like a dream.

JOHN. They commenced to drag us through the woods, and Henry was screaming and crying and raising a terrible ruckus. I told him to hush, or they'd tomahawk him, and he tried to stop, but he couldn't, the sobs just kept on coming, no matter what he did. He was scared.

HENRY. It hurt, trying to keep them back. It was like this thing in my chest that wouldn't stop trying until it got out, like a snake all balled up inside me. They smelled like sweat and dead animals from the grease on their hair. They were strong. The grip on my arm hurt.

JOHN. I tried to whisper to him not to cry, it'd be all right, we could get away somehow. But I didn't know if the Indians could understand English or not, and my Indian kept jerking my arm hard, so I decided I better shut up, but Henry wouldn't stop blubbering.

HENRY. I was eleven.

THE TALE OF THE JOHNSON BOYS

JOHN. He was slobbering out his nose. I kept seeing him how he looked when he was a baby, all red and squally, sitting there naked on the table grinning at me and throwing shit. Then I thought about Mama, and how she'd never forgive me if I let them kill him. When he was little and caterwauling about something or other I used to tell him if he didn't shut up the Indians would hear him and come in and take a scalping knife to his head. I told him stories about how the Indians would torture and mutilate you before they killed you. Now I was sorry. You're only ever sorry when it's too late to do any good.

HENRY. It was like the bad dreams I used to have when John would tell me those stories. So I thought I could maybe make it go away by closing my eyes and trying to dream about something else, but when I closed my eyes I'd fall down, and then my Indian would yank me up again and start yelling at me in Indian gibberish. The woods was like a dream now. Everything was all strange and too real.

JOHN. Mama would hate me forever.

HENRY. When it got dark and we stopped for the night, the Indians seemed to calm down and get nicer. They shared their food with us. It wasn't much, and it tasted like dirt and shoe leather, but they shared it equal. We got what they did. For some reason, that stopped me being so scared. At home we had to fight for the food on the table, and I always lost. But these Indians they shared equal with us. I thought then maybe they wouldn't kill us. Maybe they wanted to make us braves. They need more braves. They'll teach us to fight like Indians. I was getting used to the way they smelled. Truth is, they didn't smell any worse than Papa. It was just different. But not that different.

JOHN. I got to be calm and think about this, I said to myself. I got to do what John Huff would do.

HENRY. After I ate some more of it, the food tasted better to me, and I realized how hungry I was. John was quiet, eating. I could see him thinking. My Indian reached over and wiped off my chin. It was just like what Mama did. It was the same exact movement. And that was the first time I really looked at him. At his eyes. The Indian was looking at me. They were the darkest eyes. They looked holes through you. But he wiped off my chin. The fire was warm. The dark was all around us. And after a while I didn't feel so bad. It's an adventure, I thought. Me and John are having an adventure.

JOHN. After a while the Indians lay down by the fire to sleep. One wrapped his arms around Henry and the other one around me, so we wouldn't get away. There was the two Indians on either side, with Henry and me together in the middle.

HENRY. It felt warm and safe. It wasn't so bad. There was wolves in them woods, and panthers, but I felt like our Indians wasn't going to let anything bad happen to us. I went to sleep and dreamed about my sister Sally holding me and singing a lullabye. There was owls. I could hear owls. I was sleeping.

JOHN. Henry went to sleep. I kept thinking about what Mama was going through now, how the men would be getting together to try and find us. We'd gone off into the woods before and not come home for a while, and Daddy whipped me good when we got home. I waited what seemed like forever. Lewis Wetzel told me Indians never sleep, but it was a lie. Those Indians were beat. They snored like bears.

HENRY. I was dreaming about Sally washing her hair. She looked pretty, and she was singing.

JOHN. I made myself be still for a long, long time.

HENRY. Don't look at me, Henry, she said. My hair's all wet. But she was beautiful.

JOHN. After a while I managed to slip out of the Indian's arms and walked to the fire, acting like I was just going to pee. I wanted to see if they were playing possum with me. I stirred up the fire and got it going good again. I walked around the fire. Nobody woke up. I went over and whispered as quiet as I could in Henry's ear, with my lips up to his ear.

HENRY. In my dream, I wanted to touch her hair.

JOHN. Get up slow, Henry.

HENRY. What?

JOHN. Don't move fast, and don't make any noise. Slip out of his arms and get up slow.

HENRY. Why?

JOHN. Just do what I say and don't make any noise.

HENRY. Okay.

JOHN. He did what I said. He was sleepy and cranky.

HENRY. I was dreaming.

JOHN. It's time to go home now.

HENRY. They'll follow us and catch us again. They'll be mad at us then.

JOHN. They won't follow us

HENRY. Yes they will, John, and they'll catch us, too, because they're Indians.

JOHN. They're not going to follow us because we're going to kill them before we go.

HENRY. We can't kill them. What if we kill one and the other one wakes up? He'll kill us then for sure.

JOHN. We'll kill them both at the same time.

HENRY. How are we going to kill them both at the same time? There's only one gun. We can't kill them both at the same time. When you shoot the gun to kill the one, the other one will wake up.

JOHN. We'll kill one with the gun and the other with that tomahawk.

HENRY. We can't.

JOHN. Listen, Henry. We can't stand here and argue about it. They'll wake up. They're stronger than us. They're quicker than us. They know the woods better than us. The only advantage we got is right now, because they're so tired, they're sleeping and we're awake, and we're not too far from home yet. We might never catch them asleep again. They might meet up with more Indians tomorrow. We get much further away from home, we'll never find our way back. We got to kill them, Henry, and we got to do it right now.

HENRY. I don't want to.

JOHN. We got to.

HENRY. You do it.

JOHN. I can't do it by myself, Henry. Not both at the same time. You got to kill one of them.

HENRY. Can't you kill one with the tomahawk and then shoot the other one?

JOHN. The one I hit with the tomahawk might yell. If he yells and wakes up the other one we're dead. I thought it all through, Henry. You got to help me do this. And it's got to be right now.

HENRY. The Indians had left the gun leaning against a oak tree, with the tomahawks at the foot of it. John got the gun and rested it real careful on a log, with the muzzle right next to the head of my Indian, just a few inches away, so there was no way I could miss. Then he took one of the tomahawks and stood over the other Indian, and looked at me. My heart was beating something horrible. There was owls. I could hear owls. My Indian was sleeping so peaceful now. I looked back up at John. He had the tomahawk raised. He was dipping his head and mouthing one, two. I knew when he got to three I was supposed to pull the trigger. Three is a magic number. John and me always did everything on threes.

JOHN. *(Whispering the words.)* One, two, three.

HENRY. When he got to three, I closed my eyes and pulled the trigger.

THE TALE OF THE JOHNSON BOYS

(Sound of a gunshot, very loud.)

JOHN. I was worried he wouldn't do it, but he shot before I brought the tomahawk down, and I was so stunned by the sound of the shot, which was huge in the middle of the dark woods by the fire in the middle of the night, for a while I was just froze there, and something went flying. It was the Indian's jawbone, the whole bottom of his face. And then I realized Henry was screaming something at me.

HENRY. Go on. Go on.

JOHN. I was just standing there with the tomahawk above my head, straddled over this Indian, and it was like a dream, very slow, everything very slow, and Henry was screaming.

HENRY. Go on. I got this one. Go on. Do it now. John, do it now. Kill him. Kill him.

JOHN. And I saw my Indian's eyes open, and he looked up at me. And for a second we just looked each other in the eye. It wasn't fear in his eyes, or anger, or anything like that. He just looked up at me with what wasn't even a question. His eyes.

HENRY. Kill him. Kill him now. Kill him.

JOHN. And then I felt myself bring the tomahawk down as hard as I could, so hard that I missed his face, and hit him in the back of the neck, and he tried to get up, so I hit him again, and I kept hitting him and hitting him in the face and in the head with that tomahawk. It was like I was chopping wood. Once I got up a good rhythm something in me let loose, something like rage, like when Papa got drunk and went after that dog. That rage was like a dream. It was from some other place inside me. Someplace old. After a bit my arms got so tired I had to stop. I looked down and my Indian wasn't moving and his head was this bloody mess and his brains was all over my arms and face.

HENRY. I was waiting to wake up then. I think I walked off someplace, into the dark. But I don't remember it.

JOHN. I looked over for Henry but I couldn't see him. There was blood in my eyes. I could make out his Indian crawling around and moaning, the bottom of his face blown all off, like something out of a nightmare.

HENRY. I was in the dark, listening for owls. I don't know where the owls went.

JOHN. That Indian was crawling around by the fire, and I didn't want him to stumble into me, so I took off running into the dark and

92

yelling for Henry, and groping around in the weeds and bushes, and I couldn't find him, and I was screaming for him and I couldn't find him. And then I fell in a blackberry bush, and sat there, all covered with blood, and I looked up and there was Henry, sitting on a log beside me. He just looked at me.

HENRY. We should go home now, John.

JOHN. Yes.

HENRY. Mama will be so worried.

JOHN. Yes.

HENRY. John?

JOHN. What?

HENRY. Which way is home?

JOHN. I don't know, Henry.

HENRY. I don't either.

JOHN. I grabbed hold of his hand and we started to go, not running, but walking, fast and steady walking, away from the fire, away from the glow of the fire. I thought I could still hear Henry's Indian moaning back there at the fire. I just walked away from it. And I kept a tight hold on my brother's hand.

HENRY. John's hand was all sticky with something. It hurt, where he was grabbing me, but he wouldn't let go.

JOHN. We was lost for a while in the dark but then when it started to get light we recognized some of the way we'd come, a rotted out stump and a big berry bush, and then we knew where we was and we managed to make good time and get home before the sun was entirely up yet. It was faster going home.

HENRY. You got to wash up in the creek, John.

JOHN. What?

HENRY. You got to wash up in the creek before we get to the cabin.

JOHN. I can wash up at home.

HENRY. You got to wash up before Mama sees you, John.

JOHN. I didn't know what he was talking about. But when we got to the creek I looked in the water and saw my reflection.

HENRY. There was birds singing. It was morning. I knew this place. The cabin was just down the creek.

JOHN. I looked in the water and saw this person looking back at me I didn't know. I was all covered in red. I was red. The eyes looking back at me was somebody else.

HENRY. Mama'd be making biscuits.

JOHN. I put my hands in the water and tried to scrub it off. I scrubbed

THE TALE OF THE JOHNSON BOYS

at my face and my hands, scrubbed and scrubbed. The water was cold. I was cold. I was shaking. I had to get it off. I didn't want Mama to see it.

HENRY. That's enough, John.

JOHN. What?

HENRY. You washed yourself enough. Let's go home.

JOHN. So we walked down the creek to the cabin. And when we come to the door, I could smell biscuits cooking, and I heard Mama's voice saying, They're dead now. My sons are dead. They killed them in the woods. I know they did. They killed them in the woods.

HENRY. So I opened the door and walked in and says, No we ain't, Mama, we're right here, and I sure do want some of them biscuits.

JOHN. Mama just sat there at first. She thought she was dreaming. Out here, it don't often happen that you get what you want. So she half didn't believe it when she saw us. Then she come at us like a big crow and pulled us into her so hard I thought she was going to break us.

HENRY. We told them the story and they didn't believe us, which I didn't care, but it upset John considerable, not to be taken serious about it. Nobody believed we killed two Indians. You can't blame them. We was always telling stories and such, and the hardest thing for people to believe sometimes is the truth.

JOHN. Come and see for yourself, then.

HENRY. Michael Huff asked us if we could find the spot again, and John said he could. And I said we could, although I wasn't sure, myself. But I was sure of John. And Mama said, I'm not letting these boys go back out into them woods again, but the men said we should go, and John, he insisted. He wanted them to see.

JOHN. I wasn't tired any more. I had to show them. I wanted them to see it.

HENRY. So they come with us, Papa and some of the Huffs and Dickersons, and John found the way back there straight off.

JOHN. I can still see the way to that place in my sleep. I go down that path at night in my head, over and over.

HENRY. I was afraid, because everything looked different in the daytime, that maybe when we got there it wouldn't be there any more. Maybe it was a dream. And part of me wanted it to be. But not John. It was like he was angry at something. He had to show them.

JOHN. We got there and there it was, just like we left it, only different. Changed by the light.

HENRY. The fire had burned down and John's Indian was dead there by the ashes, his head all bashed in, and the bloody tomahawk there beside him where John must have dropped it.

JOHN. The men stood and looked. Now it was real for them. And I felt proud. And then, right after, ashamed.

HENRY. The other left a trail of blood we followed through the bushes. He was still alive when we found him, lying there looking up at us, the bottom half of his face gone, teeth and blood sticking out of it, looking at us, looking at me, with those same eyes, the same hand that had give me the food and wiped off my chin like Mama, clutching there kind of in my direction, just sort of, I don't know what. Like he was trying to wipe off my chin again, but couldn't reach me. He was looking at me. I just kept looking at his eyes. The Dickersons wanted to put him out of his misery, but Papa said no, he's going to die anyway, let him be. So we let him be, and went back home. I turned back to look at him once, but he wasn't looking at us any more.

(The light fades on them and goes out. Darkness.)

MOONCALF

Mooncalf: a congenital idiot; a monstrosity.

*(There is one character, REBECCA, a woman in her early seventies,
who speaks from a circle of light on an otherwise bare stage. Although she is being a letter, we do not see her writing, and there is
no desk or pen. She speaks directly to us, into the darkness.)*

REBECCA
Dear Ben—I hope you are staying warm.
It's been so cold here, like the end of the world.
My birds are keeping me busy,
and the stray cats I feed on the back porch,
and the cow calved finally out in the pasture,
the coldest night of the new year,
and Clarence said he wasn't going out there
for no damned cow in the world, on a night so cold,
with his bad back and his hernia
and his dizzy spells and his trouble peeing,
but all night I could hear the cow
mourning out there in the cold,
and I looked out the window
about three a. m., and I thought maybe
I could see her out there in the shadows
through the frost on the window
under a big January moon.
So in the morning he bundled up
and went out into the cold
and found the calf frozen dead in the snow
and the cow couldn't get up,
and Clarence started to swear
and yell at the cow to get up,
but she couldn't get up,
so he pulled her and swore some more
and kicked and yanked at her

MOONCALF

and she wouldn't get up and
wouldn't get up so
finally I put on my parka
and hobbled out over the ice
to help, and rubbed her head
and talked to her some
and Clarence pushed at her behind
and finally we got her up,
but then she wobbled and fell again
and landed on his foot,
which led to more swearing,
and he was yelling at her,
and screaming at her,
and kicking her, and yanking
at her head, and she kept
rolling her eyes over
towards where the dead calf
lay froze in the snow,
and then Clarence stopped,
and leaned against the fence,
puffing and cursing and blowing out
steam and holding his gut,
and then the cow stood up on her own
and wobbled over to sniff
at the frozen calf
and Clarence put a rope around her neck
and led her to the barn,
her legs half giving out under her.
Something was wrong with her hip,
and she was weak and all trembly.
But I got her to eat some in the barn,
and she seemed to get stronger,
and we thought she might pull through
but later in the day
she went back out
to where the frozen calf had been
and fell in the snow again
and couldn't get up.
Look at that damned stupid thing,
said Clarence.

MOONCALF

I ain't messin with that damned
stupid cow no more.
And he went into the trailer
and come out with the gun
while she looked right at him
and shot her in the head.
I didn't get no deer this year,
he says, but at least I shot me
that goddamned cow.
It was such a sad thing
it nearly broke my heart to see it.
But the silver lining in the cloud
is that now we got
all the hamburger we can eat.
I wish you would write to me
now and then. Why don't you
ever write to me? Love,
your Mother.

(The light fades on her and goes out.)

GREAT SLAVE LAKE

CHARACTERS

MARGARET QUILLER ASTOR, age 43
GRETCHEN ASTOR QUILLER, age 43
CLYDE QUILLER, Margaret's brother, Gretchen's husband, age 44
CLYDE ASTOR, Gretchen's brother, Margaret's husband, age 44
BETTY, age 19

SETTING

The front porches of two houses next to each other in the small town of Armitage, in east Ohio; in the autumn of 1938, Margaret's down right and Gretchen's down left, with just a bit of yard in the middle, and up center on a small platform two men fishing in a small boat on Great Slave Lake in Canada, a few months earlier. The set should be as simple as possible. Porch swings would be good, but chairs will do just as well.

(Sound of crickets in the darkness. Lights up on MARGARET and GRETCHEN, two women in their early forties, each sitting on her front porch in Armitage, a small town in east Ohio, on an autumn evening in the year 1938, MARGARET down right and GRETCHEN down left. Up center, in shadows at the moment, we can see the outlines of two men fishing in a boat on a lake in Canada.)

MARGARET. The worst thing is not knowing.

GRETCHEN. Yes.

MARGARET. It's waiting and not knowing.

GRETCHEN. I know.

MARGARET. I know you know.

GRETCHEN. You don't know what I know. You don't even know what YOU know.

MARGARET. I dream about them all the time. Do you dream about them?

GRETCHEN. No.

MARGARET. You don't dream about them?

GRETCHEN. I don't dream.

MARGARET. Everybody dreams.

GRETCHEN. Not me.

MARGARET. You dream. You just don't remember.

GRETCHEN. What's the difference?

MARGARET. I don't follow you.

GRETCHEN. What's the difference between not remembering your dreams and not dreaming at all?

MARGARET. There's a big difference.

GRETCHEN. What is it?

MARGARET. I don't know, but it's enormous. *(Pause.)* I dream they're up there on that lake. And it's last summer. You can hear crickets chirping in the woods, and the distant crying of the loons. *(The cry of a distant loon, as lights begin to come up on the boat.)* It's getting dark,

103

but they don't want to go back in, so they stay out on the lake a while longer.

GRETCHEN. And then what? Then what happens?

QUILLER. Do you hear that?

ASTOR. No.

QUILLER. Listen.

ASTOR. No. What?

QUILLER. Something.

ASTOR. Loons.

QUILLER. Panic.

ASTOR. What?

QUILLER. Sudden, uncanny, overpowering fear in the woods, in waste places. The prickling at the back of the neck, caused by the unexpected, irrational and overwhelming certainty that something is watching you.

ASTOR. Who is?

QUILLER. Pan.

ASTOR. Who?

QUILLER. The Great God Pan.

ASTOR. Who?

QUILLER. Panic. From Pan. He's a god who died.

ASTOR. Okay.

QUILLER. People have disappeared up here.

ASTOR. I expect.

QUILLER. Just vanished without a trace.

ASTOR. You mean on purpose?

QUILLER. I don't know.

ASTOR. Or did something come and get them?

QUILLER. I don't know. Nobody knows. It's not knowing that gets you. But then maybe you know. At the end, you know. But by then, it's too late.

MARGARET. Gretchen?

GRETCHEN. What?

MARGARET. Do you think maybe they could have just decided not to come back?

GRETCHEN. No.

MARGARET. Maybe they were just sick of us.

GRETCHEN. No. That's not it.

MARGARET. Maybe they hated us, and we just didn't know.

GRETCHEN. They didn't hate us. They loved us.

GREAT SLAVE LAKE

MARGARET. If they loved us, then something terrible has happened to them. Something dark came up out of the water, in my dream.

QUILLER. Look at that.

ASTOR. What?

QUILLER. There's something in the water.

ASTOR. Where?

QUILLER. Over there.

ASTOR. I don't see anything. What is it? A fish?

QUILLER. I don't think it's a fish.

ASTOR. What is it, then?

QUILLER. Something dark. And old, I think.

ASTOR. Like an old boot?

QUILLER. No.

ASTOR. A dead moose?

QUILLER. No.

ASTOR. What then?

MARGARET. We've always been together.

GRETCHEN. Yes.

MARGARET. Your husband Clyde. My husband Clyde.

GRETCHEN. Yes.

MARGARET. My brother Clyde. Your brother Clyde.

GRETCHEN. You make it sound like four people.

MARGARET. It is four people. You and me and my husband Clyde and your husband Clyde and my brother Clyde and your brother Clyde. Wait, that's six people. That can't be right. Oh, the math doesn't matter. I married your brother Clyde. You married my brother Clyde. We've lived next to each other all our lives. That they should go so far away and then not come back. It's unnatural.

ASTOR. We've never been this far north.

QUILLER. No.

ASTOR. Why did we come so far this time?

QUILLER. Something pulls you.

ASTOR. What does?

QUILLER. Something.

GRETCHEN. Symmetry.

MARGARET. What?

GRETCHEN. It's actually symmetry that's unnatural. There is no symmetry in the woods. Nature is chaos.

MARGARET. I don't think that's true. Nature can be orderly.

GRETCHEN. How, Margaret? How is nature orderly? Give me an

example.

MARGARET. Frost. Frost comes in wonderfully intricate patterns, like lace. That's orderly, isn't it?

GRETCHEN. That's an illusion, Margaret.

MARGARET. Frost is not an illusion. I've seen frost.

GRETCHEN. The apparent order is an illusion. Frost is actually chaos.

MARGARET. I don't see that, Gretchen. I don't see that at all. But I suppose I'll just have to take your word for it. You were always the smart one. I was just the pretty one.

GRETCHEN. I was the pretty one.

MARGARET. No, I'm pretty sure I was the pretty one.

GRETCHEN. You weren't the pretty one. I was the pretty one.

MARGARET. You mean I was the smart one?

GRETCHEN. No, I was the smart one, too.

MARGARET. You were the pretty one and the smart one?

GRETCHEN. Yes.

MARGARET. If you were the pretty one and the smart one, then what was I?

GRETCHEN. You were the other one.

MARGARET. I wasn't the other one.

GRETCHEN. If you weren't the other one, then who was it?

MARGARET. I don't know. Somebody else.

GRETCHEN. There isn't anybody else. There's never been anybody else. I wish to God there had been.

(Pause.)

MARGARET. Why do they call it Great Slave Lake?

GRETCHEN. I don't know.

MARGARET. Why did they go so far north? They never went that far north before, did they?

GRETCHEN. No. I don't think so.

MARGARET. I found it on the map. It was very far north.

GRETCHEN. Yes.

QUILLER. The Northwest Passage.

ASTOR. What about it?

QUILLER. They came up here looking for the Northwest Passage. And were lost.

ASTOR. Who was?

QUILLER. Many were lost. Uncounted numbers. Expeditions were sent out. They vanished. Just swallowed up by the woods.

ASTOR. Did they find it?

QUILLER. Find what?

ASTOR. What they were looking for.

QUILLER. Nobody knows.

ASTOR. Somebody knew. Somewhere. Sometime.

QUILLER. Maybe. But they were lost. So everything they knew was lost. Nobody knows now. Not anywhere.

ASTOR. How can you be sure?

QUILLER. About some things, a person can never be sure. About things that lead one towards despair, certainty is more likely. Death, for example.

ASTOR. And taxes.

QUILLER. I don't believe in taxes.

ASTOR. It doesn't matter what you believe. Either it's there, or it's not.

QUILLER. Clyde?

ASTOR. What?

QUILLER. Something moved over there. Something definitely moved.

ASTOR. Where?

QUILLER. I bet that water's really cold.

(BETTY ENTERS from down left, a girl of 19.)

BETTY. Excuse me. Does Clyde live here?

GRETCHEN. Clyde isn't here.

BETTY. Do you know when he'll be back?

GRETCHEN. No. I'm sorry to say I don't. Can I help you?

BETTY. I just need to speak with Clyde. It's a private matter.

GRETCHEN. You can tell me. I'm his wife.

BETTY. His wife?

GRETCHEN. Yes.

BETTY. You're Clyde's wife?

GRETCHEN. Yes.

BETTY. Are you sure we're talking about the same Clyde?

MARGARET. Which Clyde do you want?

BETTY. Is there more than one Clyde here?

GRETCHEN. There aren't any Clydes here. Both Clydes are gone.

BETTY. So there's two Clydes?

GRETCHEN. There were two Clydes.

BETTY. And they both live here?

GRETCHEN. No, one lives over there, and one lives here.

MARGARET. And one lives here.

BETTY. So there's three Clydes?

MARGARET. No, there's Clyde, Gretchen's husband, and there's Clyde, her brother, and there's Clyde, my brother, and Clyde, my husband.

BETTY. That makes four Clydes.

GRETCHEN. There aren't four Clydes.

MARGARET. We married our brothers.

BETTY. You married your brothers? Is that legal?

GRETCHEN. We didn't marry our own brothers. We married each other's brothers. My brother Clyde married Margaret. Her brother Clyde married me. So which one do you want?

BETTY. I don't know.

GRETCHEN. Do you want Clyde Quiller or Clyde Astor?

BETTY. Which is which?

GRETCHEN. I married Clyde Quiller. Margaret married Clyde Astor. I was Gretchen Astor. Now I'm Gretchen Astor Quiller. Margaret was Gretchen Quiller. Now she's Gretchen Quiller Astor.

MARGARET. I'm not Gretchen Quiller Astor. There is no Gretchen Quiller Astor. I'm Margaret Astor Quiller.

GRETCHEN. You're Margaret Quiller Astor.

MARGARET. You said I was Gretchen Quiller.

GRETCHEN. I'm Gretchen Quiller.

MARGARET. I know who you are.

GRETCHEN. You don't even know who YOU are.

MARGARET. It's very simple, dear. I'm Margaret Quiller, married to Clyde Astor, which makes me Margaret Quiller Astor, while she's Gretchen Astor, formerly Gretchen Quiller, married to her brother Clyde—

GRETCHEN. Presently Gretchen Quiller.

MARGARET. Clyde is not presently Gretchen Quiller. Don't try to confuse me.

GRETCHEN. You've been confused since 1912. Will you just be quiet and let me explain this? Two brothers, Clyde and Clyde. Two sisters, Gretchen and Margaret.

MARGARET. But not sisters to each other.

GREAT SLAVE LAKE

GRETCHEN. Not sisters to each other. Sisters to each Clyde. And each married the other Clyde brother. Have you got that?

BETTY. No.

GRETCHEN. Do I have to get out a blackboard and draw you a diagram?

BETTY. I don't think that would help.

GRETCHEN. Why is this so hard for people to understand? It seems like I've spent half my life trying to explain this.

MARGARET. Sometimes I get confused about it myself, and Clyde is my brother. I mean, of course, the Clyde who isn't Gretchen's brother is my brother. He's the one who's not my husband, which is easy enough to remember, because if Gretchen and I had the same brother, we'd be sisters, but then we'd both be married to the same person, which would not be a very happy situation, so in that respect, we're fortunate.

BETTY. Okay.

GRETCHEN. Margaret lives in a perpetual state of ambiguity.

MARGARET. I live in the state of Ohio.

GRETCHEN. For you, they're the same place.

MARGARET. I have no idea what that means.

GRETCHEN. You never had an idea in your life.

MARGARET. I had ideas once. But I've forgotten what they were. Sometimes I get up in the morning and look in the mirror and for a moment I don't know what the hell I'm looking at.

GRETCHEN. Maybe you should wear a name tag.

MARGARET. But I couldn't read it, because in the mirror everything is backwards. I suppose I could turn around.

GRETCHEN. Your head's as empty as the inside of a proton.

BETTY. Maybe I've come to the wrong place.

MARGARET. I've often had that feeling myself. Except I've never been anywhere else. Except Cleveland. Does that count?

GRETCHEN. Did you hear that?

MARGARET. What?

GRETCHEN. Listen.

QUILLER. They got wolves up here, you know, Clyde, as big as elk. Two red eyes in the dark. Come into your tent at night and rip all the flesh off your face with their teeth.

ASTOR. Is that a fact?

QUILLER. Just like Gretchen.

ASTOR. I don't think you should talk that way about my sister, Clyde.

QUILLER. You hate your sister.

ASTOR. Yes, but that's not the point. She's still my sister.

QUILLER. You're saying there's a point in having a sister?

ASTOR. I don't know what I'm saying. I don't even know what we're talking about, half the time.

QUILLER. Neither does my sister.

ASTOR. Now you're talking about my wife.

QUILLER. I'm not talking about your wife. I'm talking about my sister.

ASTOR. But they're the same person.

QUILLER. No woman is ever the same person.

ASTOR. Then who is she?

QUILLER. Somebody else. *(Sound of a loud splash.)* What was that?

MARGARET. Are we still listening? Because I don't hear anything.

BETTY. I hear crickets.

GRETCHEN. It's not crickets.

BETTY. It sounds like crickets.

GRETCHEN. I can hear the damned crickets. I'm not talking about crickets.

MARGARET. But if you say you're not talking about crickets, then aren't you talking about crickets?

GRETCHEN. Shut up, Margaret.

MARGARET. Don't tell me to shut up. You shut up.

BETTY. I really didn't mean to cause any trouble here. I just wanted to see Clyde.

GRETCHEN. What do you want to see him for?

BETTY. It's personal.

GRETCHEN. My husband had no personal relations of any kind. His life was an open book, with only about four pages. It was more like an open pamphlet. So how could you have any personal business with him? I hope you're not trying to insinuate that you were in some way involved with my husband.

BETTY. No, no, I wouldn't say involved, exactly. And I don't think it could be your husband, because the Clyde I'm looking for never mentioned anything about having a wife.

MARGARET. Well, it couldn't have been my Clyde. My Clyde loves me.

GRETCHEN. Are you saying mine doesn't?

MARGARET. I never know what yours is thinking.

GRETCHEN. You never know what anybody's thinking.

MARGARET. Nobody knows what anybody is thinking.

GRETCHEN. I know exactly what you're thinking.

MARGARET. You have no idea what I'm thinking.

GRETCHEN. You do about as much thinking as a cow.

MARGARET. How do you know what a cow's thinking?

GRETCHEN. Telepathy.

BETTY. I think I'm just going to go now.

GRETCHEN. Just stop right there, Missy. We're going to straighten this thing out, right now. You're here to see a man named Clyde, is that right?

BETTY. Yes.

GRETCHEN. A person you're not exactly involved with, who didn't tell you he was married.

BETTY. Yes.

GRETCHEN. And he didn't tell you his last name?

BETTY. It never came up.

GRETCHEN. Well, what did come up, honey? Clearly something came up. How did you know to come here?

BETTY. He said he lived on the dead end street by the old schoolhouse. This is the dead end street by the old schoolhouse, isn't it? Unless there's another dead end street on the other side of the old schoolhouse. Maybe I should just—

GRETCHEN. How did you meet this Clyde person?

BETTY. I met him at the carnival.

MARGARET. Gretchen, Clyde went to the carnival.

GRETCHEN. They both went to the carnival. Were there two of them?

BETTY. I only remember one of them.

GRETCHEN. Well, which one was it?

BETTY. I don't know.

MARGARET. I've got photographs. We'll show her photographs.

BETTY. I'm afraid that won't do any good.

GRETCHEN. Why not? Was he wearing a bag over his head?

BETTY. I don't know. I don't think so, but I can't be sure.

GRETCHEN. What are you? Some sort of idiot girl?

BETTY. No, I'm blind.

GRETCHEN. You're blind?

BETTY. Yes.

GRETCHEN. You're not blind.

BETTY. I'm legally blind.

GRETCHEN. If you're blind, then how did you get here?

BETTY. I took the bus.

GRETCHEN. How did you get here from the bus stop? Where's your cane? Where's your dog?

MARGARET. What dog? I don't see a dog.

BETTY. I don't have a dog.

GRETCHEN. How can you be blind if you don't have a dog?

BETTY. I can see shapes. I just can't make out faces. I can move through the world fairly well, with some caution, but it's like walking in fog. You know, I really think that I must have misunderstood Clyde when he said—

GRETCHEN. There it is again.

MARGARET. There's what again? The dog? I thought she didn't have a dog.

GRETCHEN. Margaret, can't you just keep your damned mouth shut for five seconds and listen for once?

QUILLER. The gazebo.

ASTOR. What?

QUILLER. It's like the voices in the gazebo.

ASTOR. What is?

QUILLER. Con used to tell me, when we were little boys, that the gazebo in our back yard was haunted. He said he could hear voices in there on windy days.

ASTOR. Who said that?

QUILLER. Con. My brother Con.

ASTOR. Con was always a strange boy.

QUILLER. Yes. *(Pause.)* I dream about him.

ASTOR. He's dead.

QUILLER. I know he's dead. You can dream about the dead.

ASTOR. It's bad luck to dream about the dead.

QUILLER. Why is that, Clyde?

ASTOR. I don't know.

QUILLER. You never liked Con.

ASTOR. He was all right.

QUILLER. You never liked him.

ASTOR. He didn't care if I liked him or not. He was too busy screwing half the women living in the state of Ohio, and probably two or three of the dead ones.

QUILLER. Con was a very charming fellow.

ASTOR. He was a dangerous son of a bitch.

QUILLER. They like that. They're excited by it. A man who carries the stench of danger around with him like a wallaby under his arm can have any woman he wants.

ASTOR. Women are insane.

QUILLER. Sometimes I forget. Sometimes I think he's going to come roaring up the driveway again, honking that damned ooga horn, with a three dollar blonde on his arm and the Devil in his eye. Con really knew how to have a good time.

ASTOR. Some people thought your brother was crazy.

QUILLER. Some people should be taken out to a distant place and shot in the head.

(Pause.)

MARGARET. Did he like walnuts?

BETTY. Walnuts?

MARGARET. Did your lover eat walnuts?

GRETCHEN. Margaret, what the hell have walnuts got to do with anything?

BETTY. I don't recall Clyde ever eating walnuts.

MARGARET. AHA!

GRETCHEN. Aha what?

MARGARET. My Clyde never ate walnuts.

GRETCHEN. So what does that prove?

MARGARET. I don't know. Something about walnuts.

GRETCHEN. It doesn't prove anything about walnuts. It doesn't prove anything about anything. This girl was involved with somebody named Clyde, who lived on a street that appears to be our street, a street on which only two people named Clyde have ever lived, as far as I know— your brother, who is my husband, and my husband, who is your brother. Now, what we need to find out here is, which husband was she fornicating with?

BETTY. I never said anything about fornicating, and I didn't know he was anybody's husband.

GRETCHEN. Don't give me that malarkey. A person could tell just by looking at him.

BETTY. I couldn't tell by looking at him because I'm blind.

GRETCHEN. We only have your word for that.

MARGARET. We could throw something at her and see if she ducks.

BETTY. Just exactly where is Clyde?

GRETCHEN. Which Clyde?

BETTY. I don't know which Clyde. Either Clyde.

MARGARET. They went fishing.

BETTY. Well, when will they be back?

MARGARET. We don't know.

BETTY. They didn't tell you when they'd be back?

MARGARET. They told us, but we don't know, because they didn't come back. They went fishing and never came back. So we don't know.

BETTY. What happened to them?

MARGARET. We don't know. Nobody knows. Well, maybe somebody knows. But nobody knows that we know of.

BETTY. That's terrible.

GRETCHEN. Why do you care? This person named Clyde you fornicated with behind the freak show tent is either my husband or her husband—which means the no good son of a bitch was deceiving you and his wife both, so why the hell does it matter to you what happened to him?

BETTY. Well, it matters to you, doesn't it?

GRETCHEN. I'm his wife. Or his sister. You are not. I have a right to know. You have no rights whatsoever in this matter. You're just a filthy little trollop.

MARGARET. Gretchen, I don't think you should talk to her like that. She's blind.

GRETCHEN. That doesn't give her a free pass to go humping around with my husband.

MARGARET. Maybe it wasn't your husband. Maybe it was my husband.

GRETCHEN. Then why are you defending her? Do you think we should let her waltz in here and tramp all over us like a couple of cockroaches just because she's blind?

BETTY. Didn't somebody look for them? Didn't they send out search parties?

GRETCHEN. They sent out search parties, but they didn't find anything. They just vanished off the face of the earth. Without a word of explanation. We just don't know. And there's no way we can know.

MARGARET. The question is, I suppose, would a person rather know, or would a person rather not know? Some people want to know the worst, no matter how bad it is. For those people, the truth makes you free, and not knowing drives you mad. For others, it's the opposite.

GRETCHEN. I want to know.

MARGARET. I thought I did, too. But now I'm not sure. In the end, of course, it doesn't really matter what you want. Or even what you know.

GRETCHEN. I don't want to know in the end. I want to know now.

ASTOR. Look at that fog coming in. This is a huge lake, Clyde. A person could get so lost out here.

QUILLER. An angler in the lake of darkness.

ASTOR. What?

QUILLER. Could be a crocodile.

ASTOR. What could? Where?

QUILLER. That thing you saw moving over there.

ASTOR. They don't have crocodiles up here.

QUILLER. Are you sure?

(Pause.)

ASTOR. Won't be able to see your hand in front of your face pretty soon. Loons. The mist rises up on the water. Like the beginning of the world.

QUILLER. Or the end.

(Pause.)

ASTOR. We should go in now. *(Pause.)* Clyde?

(Pause.)

QUILLER. Do we have any walnuts?

(Pause.)

BETTY. I can imagine what you must be going through.

GRETCHEN. No you can't.

BETTY. A person is enslaved by love. And memory. A person is enslaved by love and memory.

GRETCHEN. I'm not enslaved by anything. I just want to know what the hell happened.

BETTY. You're enslaved by your need for certainty.

GRETCHEN. You know what I think? I think you know more than you're saying.

BETTY. Everybody knows more than they're saying.

MARGARET. Not me.

GRETCHEN. Tell us the truth. We just want to know the truth.

BETTY. I met a man at the carnival. We just started talking. I liked his voice. He had a kind voice. And he was sad. He seemed to be carrying a great weight of sadness around with him. We struck up a friendship. It was really just that. Or it would have been. Except that when we said goodbye, I reached out my hand to shake hands with him, and he held my hand in both of his, very strong hands, and then he lifted up my hand and kissed it, and then he kissed me on the lips. It was the most extraordinary thing. It was very gentle. But there was such yearning in that kiss, and such infinite sadness, like a kiss from one of the damned in purgatory.

MARGARET. And you never saw him again?

BETTY. I never saw him to begin with. I'm blind.

GRETCHEN. That's a lie. It's a filthy, filthy lie. You're lying.

MARGARET. I don't think she's lying. I can tell by her eyes.

GRETCHEN. She's blind. What can you tell from a blind girl's eyes?

MARGARET. Her eyes are very expressive. And she can see some things. She can see shadows. She told us she can see shadows, didn't she? And here's something else, Gretchen. It was the carnival. Don't you remember what they used to do at the carnival?

GRETCHEN. Get sick on elephant ears?

MARGARET. They used to pretend to be each other. When amongst strangers. That's how they used to pick up girls. Pretending to be each other.

GRETCHEN. That doesn't make any sense.

MARGARET. They're men. They never made any sense. But it seemed to give them a powerful illusion freedom. Like putting on a mask. If they were somebody else, they could do whatever they liked.

GRETCHEN. Who told you that?

MARGARET. Clyde told me.

GRETCHEN. Which Clyde?

MARGARET. I forget which one. I know it was one or the other. Or maybe it was Con.

BETTY. Who is Con?

GRETCHEN. Even if they did pretend to be each other at the carnival, how does that help us? Because whichever one it was, he never told this girl he was anybody but Clyde, and a Clyde pretending to be a Clyde is still a Clyde.

MARGARET. But maybe in his mind he was pretending to be the

other Clyde. And that somehow made it all right. It wasn't really him that kissed this girl. It was Clyde. The other one. The one that wasn't him.

GRETCHEN. Margaret, that's the stupidest thing I've ever heard.

BETTY. Actually, it isn't entirely stupid.

GRETCHEN. You don't know anything about it.

BETTY. But he said something about that. About being somebody else.

GRETCHEN. He said he was somebody else?

BETTY. He said sometimes he was somebody else.

GRETCHEN. Well, who was he?

BETTY. The other one.

GRETCHEN. Which other one?

MARGARET. Did you hear that?

GRETCHEN. What?

BETTY. I think I did hear something.

QUILLER. There's something about this place.

ASTOR. What is it?

QUILLER. Things happen here that nobody sees. It all goes on without us. Caribou crossing the river. Fish swimming and mating. Pike. Walleye. Char. Muskox Pingo.

ASTOR. Muskox what?

QUILLER. You could spend a whole lifetime up here just studying the migration patterns of the birds. Packs of wolves pad through the woods at night. Red eyes in the dark at Back's Chimney. They sent out a search party, up this way, to find the Ross expedition. Just vanished. So many have vanished. And the Northern Lights. God, by the lake, have you seen it? The phosphorescence of the woods. Late at night you can hear frogs plop up onto the porch in the dark. Plop. Plop. *(Pause.)* Plop.

ASTOR. Clyde, I really think it's time to start heading back.

QUILLER. Plop.

(Pause.)

GRETCHEN. I don't hear a damned thing.

MARGARET. It sounded like a plop.

GRETCHEN. A plop?

BETTY. She's right. It was like plop. Plop.

GRETCHEN. I don't hear any plops, but the more I think about it, the more I find this mysterious blind person more than a little sinister.

She met him at the carnival, but he was somebody else. She got here by herself, but she's blind, and we can't see her dog. What has she got? An invisible dog? Where is this dog? What happened to the goddamned dog? Did she kill the dog?

MARGARET. Isn't that it, over there?

GRETCHEN. Where?

MARGARET. I saw a shape over there, in the shadows, by the ole-ander bushes. It's hard to make out for sure. It's getting dark. It could be a dog. Or a wolf. Do you see that, Gretchen?

GRETCHEN. I don't see anything.

BETTY. I don't have a dog. I'm afraid of dogs. My sister was killed by wild dogs.

QUILLER. Two red eyes in the darkness.

BETTY. I have nightmares about packs of wild dogs. They follow me at night. They have red eyes that glow in the dark.

QUILLER. River, winter, cold, oak, pine, beech, bear, wolf. These things are more real than our names.

GRETCHEN. Who are you, really?

BETTY. Well, I don't know exactly how to answer that.

GRETCHEN. I don't think you ever met my husband. I don't think you're blind at all. I think you've made all this up. You're some sort of a con artist, aren't you? You're nothing but a filthy little carny con artist.

BETTY. I'm not any sort of artist. Except I make dolls. Dolls for children. We make them and sell them. That's how we live. The blind. That's how the blind live.

ASTOR. Clyde, it's getting too dark to see out here.

QUILLER. She made dolls.

ASTOR. Who did?

QUILLER. That girl.

ASTOR. What girl?

QUILLER. That blind girl you were talking to.

ASTOR. I wasn't talking to any blind girl.

QUILLER. At the carnival.

ASTOR. I wasn't talking to any blind girl at the carnival.

QUILLER. Are you sure, Clyde?

GRETCHEN. How long have you been blind? Were you born blind?

BETTY. The blindness crept on me gradually, as I grew older. I used to read a great deal, as a child. I was ravenous for knowledge. But the more I learned, the more blind I became.

MARGARET. Some are born blind, some achieve blindness, and

some have blindness thrust upon them.

BETTY. I could make out faces, until my sister died.

ASTOR. I might have talked to a girl at the carnival. But she wasn't blind.

QUILLER. Listen to that, Clyde. There's something in the undergrowth. Moving about in the mist of the evening. Looking at us. Two red eyes. Like the eyes of a doll.

BETTY. Now I can only see remembered faces. And sometimes the faces of dolls. Everything looms up at me as if out of a terrible fog.

MARGARET. Pea soup. A pea soup fog. That's what they call it in London. Sherlock Holmes. Jack the Ripper. The world looks to her like a bowl of pea soup. And Clyde is just one of the peas. It's all better forgotten. They're gone. Why don't you come into the house, dear, and have some widow's pie?

ASTOR. Why do they call it Great Slave Lake? I didn't think there were any slaves up here.

QUILLER. There are slaves everywhere, Clyde. I should know. I married your sister.

ASTOR. Well, I married your sister. Of course, there's a big difference between your sister and my sister.

QUILLER. Really? What is it?

ASTOR. My sister isn't stupid.

QUILLER. Your sister is a monster.

ASTOR. Yes, but she has a brain. Your sister has no brain.

QUILLER. Which, I suppose, explains why she married you.

ASTOR. She married me because my sister married you.

QUILLER. But why did your sister marry me?

ASTOR. I don't know, Clyde.

QUILLER. Symmetry. The criminally insane are obsessed with symmetry. My brother Con was lucky.

ASTOR. Your brother Con is dead. How lucky could he have been if he's dead?

QUILLER. But when he was alive, he had a different woman every night. Even after he was married.

ASTOR. I know.

QUILLER. Single, married, under age, it didn't matter to Con. They were falling all over each other to get their dresses up over their heads for Con.

ASTOR. Con had a lot of energy.

MARGARET. I have a theory.

GRETCHEN. A theory?

MARGARET. Yes.

GRETCHEN. You have a theory?

MARGARET. I have a theory, yes.

GRETCHEN. About what?

MARGARET. About what happened to them.

GRETCHEN. Do you hear that, sweetheart? My friend Margaret has a theory. She has no brain, but she has a theory.

MARGARET. Do you want to hear my theory, or don't you?

GRETCHEN. I'd rather gargle motor oil.

BETTY. I'd like to hear your theory.

GRETCHEN. No you wouldn't.

BETTY. Yes. I would. I'd like to hear Margaret's theory. Why don't you want to hear it?

GRETCHEN. Because it's stupid.

BETTY. How do you know it's stupid if you haven't heard it?

GRETCHEN. Because it's Margaret.

BETTY. I think you're afraid.

GRETCHEN. Afraid of what?

BETTY. Afraid to know. Afraid to imagine. Afraid to entertain the possibility.

GRETCHEN. What possiblity?

BETTY. The possibility that she's thought of something that you haven't.

GRETCHEN. All right, Margaret. Tell us your theory.

MARGARET. No. I'm not going to tell you now.

GRETCHEN. Tell us your damned stupid theory and be done with it.

MARGARET. Say please.

GRETCHEN. I'm not saying please.

BETTY. Please.

MARGARET. I want Gretchen to say please.

GRETCHEN. Please what's your goddamned stupid theory, Margaret, you lip-diddling chowderhead?

MARGARET. My theory is, it has something to do with Con.

GRETCHEN. What could it possibly have to do with Con?

QUILLER. Who was the other passenger?

ASTOR. Who?

QUILLER. Four people in the car. My brother Con. The Pelly sisters, May and Violet, and somebody else. Three different people saw a fourth person in the car just before it crashed. But only three bodies were found. Who was the other passenger?

ASTOR. How should I know?

QUILLER. It wasn't you, was it?

ASTOR. Why would I be riding around in a car late at night with your brother Con and the Pelly sisters? I'm a married man.

QUILLER. So was Con.

GRETCHEN. I don't see what Con's got to do with it. Con's been dead for years.

BETTY. Who is Con?

MARGARET. Con is my dead little brother. Clyde's dead little brother.

GRETCHEN. Con was a no good son of a bitch.

MARGARET. You shouldn't speak ill of the dead, Gretchen.

GRETCHEN. Con Quiller was a compulsively treacherous person. Betrayal is the worst thing.

MARGARET. Bad fish is the worst thing.

GRETCHEN. Bad fish, then betrayal.

MARGARET. You're one to talk.

GRETCHEN. What do you mean?

MARGARET. You know what I mean.

GRETCHEN. I never know what you mean. You're the stupidest woman God ever made. He must have eaten some bad fish when he made you.

MARGARET. You slept with your husband's brother.

GRETCHEN. I beg your pardon?

MARGARET. You slept with my brother Con.

GRETCHEN. What in God's name ever put that idea into your head? Con Quiller is dead. I don't sleep with dead people. Except for my husband.

MARGARET. You slept with Con before he was dead.

GRETCHEN. How the hell do you know who I slept with?

MARGARET. Because he was my little brother. And you were my best friend. A person knows these things.

GRETCHEN. Con Quiller slept with anything that moved. Anything with breasts. He'd have slept with a cow if it'd let him fondle her udders.

MARGARET. So he did sleep with you?

GRETCHEN. No.

MARGARET. He slept with the cow but not with you?

GRETCHEN. I wouldn't let him sleep with me. Why are you saying these things? And what does it matter, anyway? They're all dead now.

MARGARET. We don't know that.

GRETCHEN. I wish we did know it. I wish we could know they're dead and be done with it. First there was Con, dead in that horrible burned out car with the Pelly girls, and they said there was another person in the car, but nobody knows who it was, or why it happened. And now my brother and my husband, vanished into the woods, and we don't know what happened, and we don't know why. And then this little blind bitch shows up and tries to make us believe Clyde was diddling her at the carnival, but we don't know which Clyde. I hate all this goddamned ambiguity. I just hate it. I wish somebody could tell me just one true goddamned thing, just one true thing I could hold onto.

MARGARET. You slept with your husband's brother.

GRETCHEN. You're just jealous because I'm smarter than you, and better looking.

MARGARET. I was the pretty one. I was the Queen of the Pork Festival.

GRETCHEN. And your family always looked down on me because your people had money. The Quillers had money. I married into money. And you all looked down your noses at me for it, didn't you? The Pork Festival.

MARGARET. I never looked down on you.

GRETCHEN. Well, I looked down on you. Every chance I got.

MARGARET. Why would you look down on me?

GRETCHEN. Because you were stupid. And because Harry MacBeth pulled strings with the draft board to keep your rotten brother Con out of the war so he could marry his slut of a granddaughter.

MARGARET. Con hurt his back.

GRETCHEN. How did he hurt his back? Having intercourse with the entire female population of North America? He never did an honest day's work in his life.

MARGARET. He hurt his back jumping out a window.

GRETCHEN. He was always jumping out of windows. Somebody's husband comes home unexpectedly and there's Con Quiller, jumping out the window.

MARGARET. Do you know whose window it was, Gretchen?

GRETCHEN. I don't care whose window it was. It doesn't matter. He's dead. Everybody is dead.

BETTY. I think I'm going to go now.

GRETCHEN. Don't move, bitch.

BETTY. But it's getting dark.

GRETCHEN. What the hell difference does it make to a blind person if it's getting dark or not? How can you even tell?

BETTY. I know when it's getting dark. I can feel the light draining out of the world. It's going to be very dark now. And I want to be home. I want to be home when it's dark. I'm sorry about Clyde. I mean, both Clydes. I didn't know he was married. If I'd known—I really shouldn't have come.

GRETCHEN. Then why did you? What are you really doing here? What did he do? Put a child in you? *(Pause.)* Did he? Did he put a child in you?

QUILLER. This fog is getting so thick, you can't make out anything for sure around here, can you, Clyde? It's like nothing is solid. Nothing is real. Nothing you can really hold onto. Everything begins to blend into everything else. Identity. Memory. Sanity. Time. Life and death. You can't get any objective sense of what's real and what's not.

ASTOR. Whether a person's dead or not is an objective thing.

QUILLER. Not necessarily. Not to our wives.

ASTOR. What have our wives got to do with it?

QUILLER. If you and I should disappear up here, devoured by wolves, say, or drowned in the lake, they wouldn't know if we were dead or not, would they? We might be dead, or we might have just run off to the Yukon with a couple of cute Indian girls, or one of us could be dead and the other not, but they wouldn't know for sure, and they wouldn't know which one.

ASTOR. If just one of us was dead, then the other one would go back and tell them.

QUILLER. Not if one of us murdered the other.

(Pause.)

ASTOR. Which one? Which one of us would murder the other one?

QUILLER. Which one do you think, Clyde?

(Pause.)

ASTOR. I'm cold.

QUILLER. Yes.

ASTOR. Aren't you cold?

QUILLER. Yes.

ASTOR. We got to go in now.

QUILLER. Yes.

ASTOR. It's getting very dark.

QUILLER. Yes.

ASTOR. And the fog.

QUILLER. Yes.

ASTOR. You can't see anything in the fog.

QUILLER. No.

ASTOR. You can't see your own reflection in the water.

QUILLER. No.

(Pause.)

BETTY. I really think I'm going to go now. It's getting late.

MARGARET. Don't go. Stay with us. We'll take care of you. We'll take care of your child. Gretchen and I have no children. We have no husband. We have no brother. We have nothing. Please stay with us.

GRETCHEN.She doesn't want to stay with us. For God's sake, she's carrying your husband's child.

MARGARET. Or your husband's child. And what does it matter anyway? If there's life, if she's carrying life inside her, then we need to nourish it. Treasure it. What's been left behind. I want a child. I've always wanted a child. This will be our child.

GRETCHEN. I don't want that little whore around here. Her and her screaming bastard brat. I won't have it.

MARGARET. Then she can stay with me.

GRETCHEN. She can't stay with you. I won't let her stay with you. I'll make your life hell, every day, until you get rid of her.

MARGARET. You won't say a word Gretchen.

GRETCHEN. Why won't I?

MARGARET. Because if you do, I'll tell the Sheriff who the other person in the car was, the night Con died.

(Pause. It's almost dark now. We can barely see any of them.)

ASTOR. Clyde?

QUILLER. Yes?

ASTOR. That girl at the carnival.

QUILLER. Yes?

ASTOR. Something's been bothering me about that.

GREAT SLAVE LAKE

QUILLER. What is it, Clyde?

ASTOR. She couldn't see us.

QUILLER. So?

ASTOR. So she'll never know which was which.

QUILLER. Nobody ever knows, Clyde.

(Pause. Sound of a loud splash in the water.)

ASTOR. What was that? *(Pause.)* Clyde? Are you there? Clyde?

(In the darkness, the sound of the crickets, and the distant cry of a loon. Then silence.)

Also by
Don Nigro

Joan of Arc in the Autumn
The King of the Cats
Laestrygonians
The Last of the Dutch Hotel
The Lost Girl
Loves Labours Wonne
Lucia Mad
Lucy and the Mystery of the
  Vine Encrusted Mansion
Lurker
MacNaughton's Dowry
Madeline Nude in the
  Rain Perhaps
Madrigals
Major Weir
The Malefactor's
  Bloody Register
Mariner
Mink Ties
Monkey Soup
Mooncalf
Mulberry Street
My Sweetheart's The
  Man in the Moon
Narragansett
Necropolis
Netherlands
Nightmare with Clocks
November
Paganini
Palestrina
Panther
Pendragon
Pendragon Plays
Picasso
Ragnarok

Rat Wives
Ravenscroft
The Reeves Tale
Rhiannon
Ringrose the Pirate
Robin Hood
The Rooky Wood
Scarecrow
Seance
Seascape with Sharks
  and Dancer
The Sin-Eater
Something in the Basement
Sorceress
Specter
Squirrels (Nigro)
Sudden Acceleration
Sycorax
Tainted Justice
The Tale of the Johnson Boys
Tales from the Red Rose Inn
Things That Go Bump
  in the Night
The Transylvanian Clockworks
Tristan
Uncle Clete's Toad
Warburton's Cook
The Weird Sisters
Widdershins
Wild Turkeys
Winchelsea Dround
Within the Ghostly
Mansion's Labyrinth
Wolfsbane
The Wonders of the
  Invisible World Revealed
The Woodman and the Goblins

Please visit our website **samuelfrench.com** for complete
descriptions and licensing information